Seeing Things

Seeing Things

How Your Imagination Shapes You and Your World

Rev. James P. M. Walsh, SJ, PhD

Washington, DC

New Academia Publishing, 2016

Printed in the United States of America

Library of Congress Control Number: 2015956483
ISBN 978-0-9966484-3-1 paperback (alk. paper)

New Academia Publishing
P.O. Box 24720, Washington, DC 20038-7420
info@newacademia.com - www.newacademia.com

Cover image: Rembrandt van Rijn, "Nathan Admonishing David," c1650-1655. Pen and brown ink, heightened with white gouache. Permission granted for this publication via Artstor from The Metropolitan Museum of Art, H. O. Havemeyer Collection, Bequest of Mrs. H. O. Havemeyer, 1929 (29.100.934). Photograph by Malcolm Varon. Image © The Metropolitan Museum of Art.

Editor's note: Rev. Walsh selected this painting to illustrate the story on pages 72-73, "Thou Art the Man." This painting's title was also the original title of this book, but he changed it in 2014.

Contents

University Introduction   vii
About the Author   ix

Introduction   3
1. Beginnings   5
2. What Do We Mean by Imagination?   9
3. Assumptions   17
4. Literalism   25
5. Imagining Others   35
6. Imagining the Self   41
7. What About Reason?   51
8. Selling   57
9. Imagining God   65
10. Parables   71
11. Literalism Revisited   75
12. Analogy   83
13. Re-imagining   91
14. Re-imagining God   99
15. Implications   109

Notes   115

University Introduction

In *Seeing Things: How Your Imagination Shapes You and Your World*, beloved theologian and teacher, Rev. James P.M. Walsh, S.J., shares with us the extraordinary resource of the imagination—how it animates our aspirations, our service, and a deeper connection to God and to one another. Rev. Walsh inspired all those around him to become their very best selves, and his legacy lives on through this book: his insights and reflections invite us into a greater knowledge of ourselves, our faith, and how we find our place in the world.

—*Dr. John J. DeGioia, President of Georgetown University*

Seeing Things: How Your Imagination Shapes You and Your World is a pedagogical memoir enabling the reader to enter the late Jesuit Professor Rev. James Walsh's Georgetown University classroom in various moments. Rev. Walsh considered imagination central to lived religion in the broadest sense, namely the vision of the prophet, the exegesis of the theologian, the teaching of the professor, the preaching of the pastor, and the experiences of the student, the seeker and the believer. This book stands as an eloquent and accessible mini-course in the place of imagination in moral theology, as well as the spiritual testament of a caring and loving teacher, healer, and friend.

—*Dr. David Goldfrank, Professor of History, Georgetown University*

This study is a fascinating presentation of how we imagine ourselves and the context of the world around us. Father Walsh's long-standing commitment to helping his students and colleagues understand both elevates the text to a unique level of contemplation. He was, in person, always a caring and generous man; in this effort, based on the years of teaching a course on the topic, he reveals fully just how special he was in the classroom and as a writer. This book brought back the reality of someone I always admired and the teaching ministry he pursued during the years I knew him.

—*Dr. Ronald Johnson, Professor Emeritus of History Georgetown University*

Rev. James P. M. Walsh, SJ

(Author photo by Lisa Helfert, Georgetown University)

About the Author

Rev. James P. M. Walsh, SJ was a soft-spoken but larger-than-life member of the Georgetown University community. A Jesuit priest and a full professor in the Department of Theology, he taught Old Testament and Biblical Hebrew for decades. He also co-taught "The Catholic Imagination" with a close colleague from the English Department, Dr. John Pfordresher. Dr. Pfordresher remembers Walsh developing many of the ideas found in this book during those years, as he gathered these eclectic, wide-ranging, and often wittily funny examples. From 2009-2012, Walsh joined the faculty at Georgetown's campus in Doha, Qatar, demonstrating his nuanced and engaged commitment to interfaith dialogue in the Middle East and globally.

Students admired Walsh as a consistent, passionate voice for a well-rounded, liberal undergraduate education. "How happy he was that I chose to study Shakespeare and music, not only government, economics, and history," recalls former student Max Coslov. He encouraged students to question assumptions and strive to be more compassionate, doing so with few words and mostly by his living example. Another student, Nikolai Wenzel, recalls Walsh's religious influence: "He taught me about imagination, about seeing the other, and about serving friends. I left the Church some years ago, but it seems to me that imagination (a precursor to love, perhaps) was Christ's central message. Father Walsh always taught that message, directly and through stories, woven with Christianity or not, and it has been one of my most valuable life lessons." Wenzel remembers Walsh leading a supper roundtable known as "Tales," where a dozen young men would break bread and share stories while he encouraged them to engage creatively beyond their majors.

For four decades Walsh was the Jesuit member of the Georgetown Chimes, an internationally recognized a cappella singing group founded in 1946. His title was "Celestial Chime," and former student Rosario Conde said she and others claimed he had a mystical quality that was evident when he sang or even casually hummed. His scholarship, singing, companionship and very presence, Chimes say, comprised an extended reverence to the majesty of God. His own most memorable Chimes experience was at his profession of final vows in the Jesuits in 1982, when Chimes sang during the Mass in Dahlgren Chapel. Students admired his musical range, from studying classical guitar and singing in classical choirs to snapping his fingers and guiding his young charges in such popular styles as Barbershop.

"Have you ever met anyone else who understands Cyriac and Ugaritic?" asks Coslov, and indeed, Walsh's language capabilities comprised much of his legend. "Being with Jim you couldn't help but become a fellow lover of language and etymology, and his eyes sparkled when thinking about the origins and meaning of words." Wenzel adds that he taught himself Russian at the age of forty, and "picked up Spanish and French somewhere along the way."
Patrick McKegney writes, "Many will speak of [him] as a mentor, a brother, a father, or a spiritual guide. Some will call him all of the above. But most important, he was a friend. Your brilliant friend who put up with all of your crass jokes and misplaced sense of self-importance. Your friend who taught you that the world was bigger than the two feet in front of you. He was an endless sea of knowledge that could be generously shared if you just took the time to listen. And he was a patient teacher. When I was still a student, I asked him how he could know so much and still believe in God. He didn't chastise or criticize, judge or joke. He simply turned to me and said 'Why does there have to be a disconnect between understanding and faith?'"

He may be considered the consummate educator, but he was also a perpetual student, one who made a cornerstone of his career the art of looking at the world through other people's eyes. In many ways he embodied liberal learning, challenging and encouraging students to take more classes in the humanities, and to seek coherence in their educations. Georgetown's Jesuits hope that the fruits of their dedication to learning and service will be *Ad Majorem Dei Gloriam*: to the greater glory of God. But as Conde sums it up, "It is people like Father Walsh who teach all of us what this looks like and also how we can do this in the ordinary circumstances of our own lives."

Editor's note: Rev. Walsh's original "About the Author" was much shorter, and in Jesuit style said little about himself. I urged him to at least let others tell us more. He offered some student names, they generously answered my questions, and that is how this more narrative "About the Author" came to be. This version was comprised of memories of Dr. John Pfordresher, Ms. Rosario Conde, Mr. Max Coslov, Mr. Patrick McKegney, Mr. John Stewart, and Dr. Nikolai G. Wenzel. Mr. Mark Ouweleen consulted on it. Walsh was able to read some of their comments in an earlier version, and they made him laugh. However, he surely would have preferred his original, shorter statement.

He began working on this book some years ago, and he continued to rework it almost until his death. As the director of Georgetown's Office of Scholarly Publications, I became involved in early 2014. We worked together to create a proposal to submit to publishers. Although, unfortunately, Walsh passed away before a publisher was secured, I am delighted that Dr. Anna Lawton of New Academia Publishing has produced this lovely edition. At his death the manuscript was nearly but not quite complete. I have edited some portions of it in ways I believe reflect his keen intelligence and wit, his great love for his students, and his wishes. The full and unedited version is available in his archive in Lauinger Library. My thanks to Dr. John Glavin of Georgetown's English department for consulting on this edition, and also to Dr. John Pfordresher for essential context on how this book came to be.

—*Dr. Carole Sargent, Director, Office of Scholarly Publications*
Georgetown University

Seeing Things

Introduction

At the beginning of each semester a trail of students from the previous semester makes its way to my office. In almost every case, they come to complain about the grade they received in my course. Naturally I decline to discuss their grade but I do take the opportunity to congratulate them for the courage they show in opening themselves to a review and critique of their performance in the semester previous. It takes courage to look squarely at one's choices, especially when those choices are wrong ones (as indicated by the analog indicator of performance we call grades).

In some cases, my congratulations are well placed: as we go over their work, especially the final exam, they see and acknowledge how they missed the point, or conflated unrelated matters, or failed to see connections, or skipped studying. I admire these students for their intellectual generosity.

In other cases, though, all they want to talk about is that analog indicator, the final grade. Our review of the final, to them, might as well be Snoopy going "Wah wah wah." They keep returning to their bottom line: "I am a good student. I am an A student, not a C-minus student."[1] All in the full-blown tragic mode.

I have come to the realization, after many years, that they are expressing an unshakeable conviction. No evidence avails to counter it. And that conviction resides not in their rational faculties but in the imagination. It is deep within them, and carries a powerful weight of emotion.

1

Beginnings

Years ago I had a visit from a former student who is now involved in law enforcement. He told me that his job required him to prosecute marijuana growers and that he felt somewhat hypocritical about it: as a student he had "experimented" with weed and yes did inhale. So he did some research about cannabis and its effect on neurological development, especially the teenage brain.

He pursued further reading about brain development, and as we chatted he sketched some of what he had found. At puberty there is a kind of growth spurt in the development of the frontal lobes—a slow-motion spurt, to be sure, since it doesn't end until one's twenties. Marijuana has a hugely harmful effect on that development in adolescents, as does alcohol.

In some ways that development of the frontal lobes is what makes us fully human. It allows us to project a future, envision consequences of choices and actions, and put ourselves imaginatively in the place of another.

Projecting a future: as we talked I thought of the heart-breaking fact of teenage suicide. A fifteen-year-old (say) is deeply depressed, and friends and family and teachers offer comforting words. "Hang in there: it won't always be like this, you'll see." But though the kid knows the meaning of the words, they won't get through. Physiologically, in terms of neurological development, that young person is literally incapable of really understanding them. That fifteen-year-old brain is not yet at the point where it can project a future in a meaningful way.

Another vaguely remembered snippet of conversation came back to me from many years before—perhaps it had to do with the work of Jean Piaget. What I recalled was a story of three brothers, let's call them Tom (10), Dick (7), and Harry (4). The conversation goes like this. "Harry, do you have any brothers?" Yes, Harry says, Tommy and Dickie. "How old are they?" Harry tells you, ten and seven. "Harry, does Tommy have any brothers?" Furrowing of brow, shrugging of shoulders.

The conversation with my law-enforcement friend made sense of that story: it's the frontal lobes that make it possible for us to put ourselves in the place of another. Harry's four-year-old brain wasn't there yet. He couldn't imagine the world as his brother sees it. I remembered the game of hide and seek when I was "found" hiding behind a tree trunk, and the sense of unfairness I felt so deeply: if I couldn't see the kid who was "it," counting to a hundred with his eyes closed, how could he now see me? (When this happened I was considerably older than four.)

Those were not my only reactions to what my friend told me from his reading about brain development.

I thought of what we college teachers experience in our work with eighteen-to-twenty-two year olds. They come to us as let us say works in progress and four years later they are or seem to be fully formed, among our dearest friends and companions. So what exactly is it that *we* are doing, if that brain development takes place all on its own? Is it make-work, wasted effort?

No, my friend assured me. Without the stimulus of stories, songs, movies, poetry, history, the experience of work in the lab— without all that, the development of the prefrontal cortex would not take place. (Think of children put to work in the fields or the mines and the look they have as they age, the vacant stare, the lack of quick responsiveness and alertness.)

No, our work as teachers is crucial in our charges' neurological development.

That conversation thirty years ago started me on the study of the imagination and, from that study, the course on imagination that I have offered for over two decades now. Brain science has developed so rapidly, and continues to develop in what seems to be exponential progress, that while I have followed it as a layman it would be presumptuous to offer anything more than some of what seems already to be established.

At the beginning of the imagination course, a psychiatrist friend of mine comes in to class to lecture on the brain and brain development: Brain Science 101. 100 billion nerve cells, each of which contacts at least 10,000 other nerve cells; circuitry and distributed systems; the limbic system; the prefrontal cortex (the story of Phineas Gage); why puberty is so difficult. Students who have younger siblings especially like this quotation, from Thomas Gualtieri, M.D.:

> The fully developed but prepubertal child, age 10 or 11 years, is one of the supreme creations of nature, and a walking example of the extraordinary capacities of the corpus striatum. He or she has developed a full range of adaptive behaviors and is fully capable of independent action, even in complicated, modern societies . . . has mastered the skills of reading and calculation—arts that [it] has taken the species a thousand centuries to develop—and can use those skills to master new, more complicated endeavors. . . . understands social relationships and builds his or her own social structures, which are sometimes extraordinarily subtle and complex, and does it all with good cheer, deference to his or her elders, and a moral sense that is sometimes painful to the adults they live with. Moralistic may be an appropriate word.[2]

Perhaps the students remember themselves at that stage of growth; their parents surely do, with fondness. What happens in puberty can be painful and confusing for all, but an understanding of how the brain works can help to understand what is causing it, and it has to do with that prefrontal development. More recent research has suggested that that development is not complete until one is pretty far into one's twenties, not early twenties as had been thought. And studies of brain plasticity suggest that brain development is not a matter of straight-ahead rigid programming.[3]

Then there is a radio piece by Kurt Andersen, relating how a University of California study tested four stroke victims.

> The strokes had injured one particular small area on the left sides of the victims' brains—but otherwise left their minds in perfect operating condition.

And as a result, they were able to intelligently discuss and understand everything—except metaphors.

This metaphor study was low-tech. The researchers simply read 20 metaphorical statements and proverbs to the stroke victims. Like 'The grass is always greener on the other side' and 'A rolling stone gathers no moss.'

And with almost every metaphor they were read, the patients could respond with only very, very literal interpretations. For instance, they thought that 'All that glitters is not gold' meant that we have to beware of unscrupulous jewelry salesmen. One of the researchers' lines was 'George Bush isn't exactly a rocket scientist, is he?' And the patients replied that the statement simply meant that President Bush is a politician, and isn't involved in aeronautical design at all.

Which is sweet and sad—and amazing that this one particular bit of the brain, a bit of tissue just above and behind the left ear, is the part of our hard wiring that lets us understand Shakespeare, to fully comprehend poetry, literature, and art—that lets all of us intellectually reach for the stars.

And as a matter of fact, 'reaching for the stars' was one of the sayings that the patients in the study simply didn't get.[4]

There is more to say about literal mindedness, but Andersen's account is a compelling point of reference. Not all literalism is due to neurological damage.

2

What Do We Mean by "Imagination"?

Every man possesses in a greater or lesser degree a talent, which is called imagination, the power of which is the first condition determining what a man will turn out to be, for the second condition is the will, which in the final resort is decisive.[5]

—Søren Kierkegaard

As in the course so here, the first thing is to sort out the various ways we use the words "imagination," "imagine," "imaginary," and "imaginative." (Throw in "re-imagine" and you have a GE commercial.) Doing this in-class exercise most students responded to the verb "imagine" by citing the John Lennon song (which arguably indicates a kind of Pavlovian response).

Some sentences show the range of meanings of the notion:

I couldn't begin to imagine how people could do such a thing.
When I was a child I had an imaginary friend.
Whoever plans the menus isn't very imaginative.
I think she imagines herself as Norma Desmond.
You only imagined it.
Why didn't U.S. Intelligence foresee 9/11? A failure of imagination.
They imagine the other side as evil incarnate.
Our Lady of Guadalupe Mass without Mariachi music? Unimaginable!
He imagines two classes of people in America, "makers" and "takers."

They let their imaginations run riot.
Churchill's "Iron Curtain" was an imaginary line—until 1961.

Reviewing the 1975-76 exhibition "The European Vision of America," J. H. Elliott combines these variants of the notion in one paragraph (emphasis added):

> The exhibition tells us something about America, . . . But it tells us a great deal more about Europe and **the European imagination**. . . . Medieval **images** of the terrestrial paradise, . . . and of the golden age described by the authors of classical antiquity, intermingle with **images** of amazons and anthropophagi, drawn from the **imaginative** pages of the possibly **imaginary** Sir John Mandeville.[6]

To narrow the question, let's say the verb and the noun have to do with mentally depicting or representing:

He imagines life as a Frank Capra movie.
Often sex workers can't imagine leaving "the life" behind.
I've always imagined the Catholic Church as a finger-wagging nanny.
Cooking meth in his college dorm room? I guess he imagined it was a good idea.
Gandhi perhaps imagined the British would respond well to non-violence.
He imagines other people as "brutal and untrustworthy."
Lost in her texting she walked into traffic. Did she imagine she was alone in the world?
He imagined a rock in every snowball.
Their imaginative world is that of Quentin Tarantino.

But here a distinction is in order. It is useful to note two ways the imagination works, what I call instrumental and spontaneous. The first is captured in the phrase "use your imagination"; the second might be expressed as "free your imagination."
Here is an exercise in "using" your imagination.

Picture yourself sitting in a room. The room is dark. No sounds from outside break the surrounding silence. Then you hear footfall. Someone is ascending stairs. The sounds get nearer. You hear the door to your room open and you see someone standing there. In the light from outside the room you see a tall young man. He is wearing the uniform of a United States Marine—the dress uniform. He has red hair. He stands at attention in the doorway.

Did you manage that exercise all right? Step by step, as the details came out you pictured them, and yourself as experiencing them. You used your imagination. (This is what happens when we fantasize, except that we ourselves are writing the script and are in control.)

Now, to show the difference between that (instrumental imagination) and what I am calling spontaneous imagining, try the following exercise.

You are sitting in a room. The room is dark, and very quiet. As you sit there you hear someone coming up the stairs, getting closer and closer. The door opens, and framed in the light you see—

Who comes spontaneously to mind? That is up to you, but if it really is spontaneous imagining you have no say about it. You are not in control. In class we do not "go there," since for each student the figure framed in the light might well be someone associated with deep fears or deep longing, and that is too personal to talk about—not in class anyway.

Where does that spontaneous image come from? Chances are it will carry with it strong affect, feelings one has perhaps been unaware of. That level of image and emotion is what this book is about.

Further, the imagination is the repository of all sorts of impressions and assumptions, a picture of the world and of others and of oneself, and it controls our thinking.

A trusty example of this is what by now is an old chestnut, one that has been around for decades—recently I saw it among a set of riddles for young children—but is still useful for purposes of the course. It consists of a brief story, and the listener's or reader's reaction to it.

A man and his son are out driving and get into a terrible accident. They are taken to the emergency room of the nearest hospital. The driver (the father) has suffered only minor injuries and is released, but the son is severely injured and requires immediate surgery. He is taken into the operating room (O.R.). The surgeon on duty walks into the O.R., and seeing the patient says, 'I cannot operate on that boy. He is my son.'

Many people react to the story with puzzlement: how can that be? We have already been told that the father was treated and released, so how could he . . . And so on. (I remember how a colleague shared in that same puzzlement, a colleague who teaches a course in feminist theology.)

There is nothing in the story, or the way it is told, to cause puzzlement. Not at all. The reaction comes from one's imagination, and one way to bring this out is to go to "thinking" and ask, "Are all surgeons male?" Of course not . . . oh. When one hears "surgeon," though, the image that comes through is of a man, and that image controls how one hears the story. Now, *that* is spontaneous imagining.[7]

As we begin the semester, then, we explore various aspects of the imagination, not so much by thinking about it but by in-class experience, spending some time on what we often see in others, if not in ourselves: Failure of Imagination.

If development of the frontal lobes is what enables one to put oneself imaginatively in the place of another, or to enter imaginatively into a different setting or a future, failure to do so can reasonably be called a failure of imagination. The students are asked to write up some incident where such a failure might be thought to occur, whether they merely observe it or are themselves involved.

Last year one student wrote about a volleyball match where the opposing team stuck to its game plan even when they were losing badly. Instead of adjusting to what our team was doing, they kept on doing the same, losing thing. Apparently it never occurred to the visiting team to do anything other than what they had learned in practice. The class agreed that that was a good example of "failure of imagination."

Another example elicited general agreement, though not from me. In the comic strip "For Better or For Worse," Elizabeth, the teenage daughter of the family, is having lunch in the cafeteria with her classmate Duane at the beginning of the school year, discussing what they did during the summer. Duane has a Mohawk haircut and multiple piercings, and chews his food with his mouth open. He tells Elizabeth he spent the summer working for his dad: "For some reason, I couldn't get a job."

Was there a failure of imagination at work here? The class was virtually unanimous that there was—on the part of prospective employers! Interviewers couldn't get beyond the Mohawk and the nose ring and the tongue stud, to see the person underneath with his (presumably) fine qualities.

But a few students allowed as how maybe Duane himself might be said to exhibit a failure of imagination: it didn't occur to him to consider how he might appear to the interviewer. He never imagined that the way he presents himself to the world at large might be off-putting. And (I would say) perhaps the true failure of imagination consists in this, that "the world at large" has never become part of Duane's imaginative world.

What in this exercise—as in many others throughout the course—interested me was that the students spontaneously identified with the teenage character. Perhaps they share the same imaginative world.

Writing this I have found a memory coming back, of a time when I was guilty of a failure of imagination. It was the summer between freshman and sophomore years of high school. I was visiting my sister, who lived in Washington D.C. She met up with a friend who had a son a few years younger than I was and the four of us set out, in the sweltering summer heat, to find relief in a local swimming pool. The attendant told us that my sister and I could use the pool but my sister's friend and her son could not. They were

African-American (Negroes, in the usage of 1952). Well, fine, that didn't affect me. I went swimming.

Some failures of imagination are shameful.

Another exercise. Every teacher knows that the best teaching happens when you get the students talking among themselves. They do, mostly, listen to one another. So I would divide the class randomly into five or six groups of a few each and give each group one case presented in the syndicated "Carolyn Hax" column. After each group has come to a consensus on how to understand the problem presented it, and the advice to be given the letter writer, we move to a general discussion. I read aloud the letter Group One has been discussing, students in the other groups comment off the top of their heads, and finally one student from Group One reports on what they have agreed is the best way to respond. Then on to Group Two, and so on.

In effect they are playing Carolyn. In so doing, they have an experience of adult life. Though they understand they are not to take a judgmental or condemnatory approach, they still are put in the position of assessing the choices and attitudes of another person, in an objective and disinterested but, I hope, not self-distancing way.

Most often the groups come up with the same response as Carolyn Hax, though when I finally read hers to them they are taken aback at her candor. They could not imagine themselves saying, "Grow up!"—maybe because they have heard that counsel themselves throughout their teenage years—but that is the kind of thing Carolyn can unfurl.

At this point it helps to gather together what we have so far seen and try to sort things out. A friend of mine once suggested a way of schematizing various levels of the psyche, and that three-level "map" of the psyche—though vastly oversimplified—is what we use throughout the course.

> At the *surface* of consciousness is the 'blooming, buzzing confusion' of everyday life. Some things and persons may swim into explicit awareness and the rest of what is around us becomes background noise. Then awareness changes, and something else engages our attention. And so on.

At a deeper level, something may engage our attention and in focusing on it we *think* about it. This is the level of reasoning, ratiocination, specific and explicit intellectual engagement. It may involve puzzlement but we want clarity, insight, so we 'think it through.' We might have a eureka moment, but that may be followed by the reflex question, 'Is that really so? I wonder . . .' If we embrace the insight we have arrived at, we can give reasons for doing so. All is explicit and, ideally, clear. This is the level of thinking, of reason.

A third level is the part of the psyche I call imagination, in the sense of 'spontaneous' imagining discussed above. Vivid images, powerful feelings swirl around, or lie dormant, in reserve as it were, and they escape intellectual scrutiny for the simple reason that we are unaware of them. Other people, however, experience them as they come out in what we say and do. The rest of this book will offer many examples of this dynamic.

"The sleep of reason produces monsters." I have always wondered what kind of genitive that is, subjective or epexegetic. Does "the sleep of reason" mean dogmatic slumber that closes off access to that level of feeling and image we are dealing with here?

Two comments are in order. I have found that some students spontaneously begin to refer to this third level, the imagination, as "the subconscious," and I have to caution them not to assume any kind of equivalence, for two reasons. The first is that Freud's "map" of the psyche has its own integrity and theoretical foundation; and to make careful distinctions—avoiding facile equivalences—is a habit of mind to be esteemed and cultivated. The other reason is that students seem, nowadays, to resist accepting anything that to them is "new," as in the reaction "Yeah, I know that." "We had that in high school." They do not seem to know that intellectual delight comes from ignorance—*not* knowing something—so that the joy of discovery can be theirs.

Now let us look at "assumptions": how they are rooted in, and reveal, the workings of imagination, and the role they play in creating the reality we live in. Then, the phenomenon of literalism, cognate as it is in many respects with the role assumptions play in shaping our reality.

And in subsequent chapters, how people imagine others and imagine themselves—and the ironies inherent in the tensions between levels two and three.

3

Assumptions

As the example of the surgeon suggests, our images of reality determine what we hear and how we hear it, all unbeknownst to us ourselves.

How many years, even generations, did Crayola include in their boxes of crayons one called flesh-colored? No one realized that flesh is not necessarily pink—no one, that is, who looked like me. Assumptions led to failure of imagination; or is it the other way around?

In traffic, we assume that other drivers will stay in their lane, wait at intersections until they can turn safely, pay attention to what they are doing, and even perhaps use their turn signals. Or, maybe, we anticipate none of these things because we have experience of bad drivers. Or, indeed, we can't imagine other drivers *not* acting responsibly because we ourselves would never dream of doing anything but these things—which makes us bad drivers. In any case, our anticipations and subsequent actions are rooted in assumptions, and those assumptions come from how we imagine other drivers behave. After the accident the one driver will say, "Well, I assumed the other car would . . ." Yes. In the driver's imaginative world, that assumption makes perfect sense. And it keeps body shops in business.

Not only on the road but in parking lots as well assumptions come into play. If a car occupies a disabled-parking space and no appropriate sticker, tag, or license plate is visible, people become irate and sometimes will challenge the driver. Later, after the altercation, one will hear, "Well, he didn't *look* . . .." Which is to say, he didn't look like what I imagine disabled people look like.

Friends from California told me about a pile-up of a hundred and two vehicles on California route 99 a few years ago. Tooling along at their usual rate of speed drivers encountered the dread, and rare, Tule fog—something they never imagined might happen. Instead, they imagined—well, driving, and they didn't slow down. They assumed that driving as usual would work.

I once gave a talk at a prestigious college preparatory school to a small group of students about something or other in my field of expertise, the Old Testament, and the first question I got was, "Why are you so different from the priests in our parish?" The question came from certain assumptions about priests, how they look and how they talk and (I guess) what they think. I forget what I said in response, but the memory of the question the student asked and the life-long church-going experience that I assumed her question reflected has stayed with me.

(Yes, it was a girls' school—did you imagine something else when you read "a prestigious college preparatory school"? Again, assumptions.)

Another example: Former member of the U.S. House of Representatives Pat Schroeder (D.-Colorado) tells how she was turned away from the Congressional parking area because the attendant assumed she was a secretary: "You don't look like a Congressman," he said.

Not just women: African Americans know well the determinative power of assumptions. "He didn't look like a professor." "I thought he was maybe dangerous." You go into a store and feel the eyes of the salespersons following you around. A woman clutches her purse closer to her as you pass her on the street. People are exaggeratedly agreeable in your interactions with them. Lots of assumptions there.

Sometimes assumptions are fatal.

[In Guatemala in the second half of the twentieth century] the army had several *a priori* assumptions about who were insurgents, either as combatants or collaborators. Any person described by one or more of these assumptions immediately became suspect and usually marked for torture and death. There was no attempt to establish innocence or guilt.

. . . For an extended period of time, people simply did not believe the army was acting as blindly and ruthlessly as it actually was in carrying out its counterinsurgency plan. In the testimonies time and time again people originally believed the army was considering each individual case, was trying to make reasonable judgments about the innocence or guilt of individuals and had arrived at mistaken conclusions perhaps based on false information from *orejas* (spies). Community elders or the parish priest would try to reason with soldiers carrying out abductions or executions, or perhaps go to see the regional army commander to try to explain an alternative view. The army's automatic assumption was that the people they had seized were subversives and that anyone who attempted to intervene on their behalf must also be aligned with the guerrillas in some fashion. Consequently they also were usually marked for torture and death.[8]

Here we have two sets of assumptions: those of the army and those of the elders or clergy who tried to intercede on behalf of those the army targeted. The intercessors assumed that the army's heart was in the right place, and that their arrests were based on evidence, judiciously weighed. The army assumed that the campesinos—poor, dark-skinned—were subversive if not insurgents, and that anyone who was on their side was *ipso facto* a revolutionary.

Another realm where assumptions are determinative until brought to light and challenged is school, as I have found in my line of work. Students come with expectations of learning based on their previous experience. If they have never experienced the delight of discovery, making connections, achieving insight, then their expectations will be accordingly minimal, and everything in curriculum and classroom that does not meet their expectations— their sense of what is important and significant—will be simply disregarded. "Whatever" / "Same old same old" / "Will that be on the final?" Many of the students in the school where I teach are so bright they got through high school without much effort, and assume the same will be the case in college. Very many have gone through their previous schooling by passing standardized exams and getting high grades, and they assume that will be true here as well. For a distressing number of students, intellectual activity has consisted in using an internet search engine to get answers to questions, an experience that has resulted in two related phenomena: they assume that the point of education is to get information; and they see no need to actually *know* things. Hence, they assume that intellectual activity is pointillist, involving "facts" unrelated to any larger world, rather like answers on television's "Jeopardy"; and since understanding is a matter of making intelligible connections, and they have no store of knowledge to bring to bear on material not previously encountered, they cannot think. In their imaginative world, deriving from this kind of high school experience, that is what education is, and that is what they as students are expected to do, and that is who they are; and from this (unarticulated) self-image come the assumptions they bring to college.

Americans teaching in other countries around the world will face assumptions different from what we are used to. The model elsewhere seems to consist of information imparted and digested and then reproduced in examinations. There is no give and take, no questioning—apart from "How do you spell that?" or the like— much less challenging, as our schooling at its best expects.[9] The assumptions that determine how Church officials exercise their teaching office seem to derive from this kind of educational experience, and their expectations of how the faithful will receive official teaching accord with those assumptions. Think of the delighted reactions of the audience in late-night television infomercials.

Jonathan Mirsky has spelled out the assumptions that underlie American foreign policy. We are "champions of freedom," and (not to mention the question-begging involved in that word "freedom") there is

> a potent self-image as a unique people destined by geography, history, and moral character to guide politically immature and easily misled [peoples] to a better future...[combined with a] strong sense of exceptionalism and destiny....[10]

While it is tempting to ascribe these convictions to the late nineteenth century, beginning with America's takeover of the Philippine Islands, a similar self-image and corresponding assumptions can be seen in a report sent to Rome in the early seventeenth century, recounting how the Jesuit missionary John Altham addressed the chief of the Piscataway Indians in southern Maryland:

> when the Father explained, as far as he could through the interpreter . . . the errors of the heathen, [the chieftain] would, every little while, acknowledge his own; and when he was informed that we had come thither, not to make war, but out of good will towards them, in order to impart civilized instruction to his ignorant race, and show them the way to heaven, and at the same time with the intention of communicating to them the advantages of distant countries, he gave us to understand that he was pleased at our coming.[11]

The Piscataway leader was clearly a man of great courtesy and tact.

In speaking of prejudice and prejudices we are speaking of assumptions, as those assumptions are rooted in the ways we imagine the world. One set of assumptions especially makes me cringe, since it touches closely my life, with its experience and choices. Here, from Norman Cantor's history of the Black Death, is an unadorned example:

> Religious authorities, whether priests or rabbis, are always in the front ranks of celebrants of the marriage of the scions of rich families. It was and is an appearance they relish making, and not just because of the succulent gifts that they will receive from the families involved. They are happy to perform ceremonies in festive and lavishly decorated surroundings that the rich and powerful own.[12]

Eamon Duffy comments:

> Cantor becomes particularly dismissive whenever he deals with clergy, for whom he seems to have a particular loath-

ing. So he tells us that the prime concern of abbots was "force-feeding the fat monks," bishops "mumble" their sermons, even when preaching before kings, bloated popes wash down "exquisite and lengthy feasts" with fresh Rhone wine.

The assumptions given voice in Cantor's book do seem to result in a fun-house-mirror image of medieval life. Again, from Duffy's review:

> For all their undoubted raciness, Cantor's Middle Ages come across as alien and repellent, a moral freak-show, where virtually nobody has high ideals or human decency, almost nobody does their job well, almost nobody deserves our respect. If you think that the past was peopled by grotesques and gargoyles, that virtually all priests were sycophantic gluttons, all peasants downtrodden, all landowners brutes, all kings tyrants—if you think that every motive was base, every relationship exploitative, every marriage a conveyor belt for property or a joyless machine for making (male) babies—you will probably enjoy this book.

In a sense, all the examples given above come down to what we saw in the surgeon story. The way we experience and understand an event or interaction or policy is founded on certain assumptions, and those assumptions are rooted in the imagination, as the imagination has been shaped by previous experience—experience that itself is shaped by the same assumptions.

Yet this Moebius strip—assumptions determining experience, experience reinforcing assumptions—must have a beginning somewhere, in a set of images and emotions the more powerful because (as I will be suggesting) they are rooted in early life.

But there is one more aspect of this matter that in the course we treat upfront. Why is it people fail to "get it"? In these troubled times, from Africa to Southwest Asia, and in redoubts of America itself, the media focus on "fundamentalism." I prefer to use the historically and epistemologically more accurate term "literalism." The next chapter will get us started on the question.

Then, as promised, we look at the various ways people imagine others and then (what is trickier) how people imagine themselves—and the attendant anomalies of that imagining.

4

Literalism

Part of what it means to suffer a failure of imagination may be that one can't conceive that one's imagination is impoverished.[13]

—H. Allen Orr

In the first chapter I quoted Kurt Andersen's account of the lingering effect of strokes on some patients: they were deprived of the ability to understand metaphors. Not all such incapacity, however, is the result of neurological damage, or so it seems. Think of children. A friend told me how when his mother served calves liver for dinner, urging the children to eat it because "It has iron," little Otto would poke at the meat on his plate looking for tiny iron fibers or filings.

A student told the class how his sister, whose nickname was Baby (she was the youngest child in the family), was distressed when she learned that she would have a new younger sibling—she heard the family excited about having a new Baby! Baby the common noun, "Baby" the proper name: she couldn't distinguish.

A little boy in a family I know was taken to see *Jaws* when it first came out in the summer of 1975. He was very quiet on the ride home, until finally he said, "I'm glad they got that shark, cuz we're going to Ocean City next week." Tommy did not distinguish between his life and the world he had just seen on the silver screen: it was all an undifferentiated one.

To those sample stories you the reader could easily add more—at least, if we are talking about children. What about grown-ups who take things literally?

Well, some people are self-centered. The distinguished writer Tony Kornheiser tells this story about a woman who was laid up at home after minor surgery.

After a few days the household food supply dwindled, [so] she phoned her husband at work and . . . mentioned there was nothing in the house to eat.

"No problem," her husband said, "I'll eat out."[14]

Then there is the story about the residence for graduate students where I lived many years ago. Every Tuesday breakfast was pancakes, but every Tuesday the syrup was put on the table chilled. A group of residents went to the man in charge to ask if the cook could take the big can of syrup out of the refrigerator Monday evening so in the morning the syrup could be room-temperature. Or even, possibly, warmed? His response: "I don't take syrup." This reply was widely viewed as indicating remarkable self-centeredness—or at least a narrow focus, with much in common with literal-mindedness, as in this next example.

A few years back, a New York dance company mounted a production of Stravinsky's *Histoire du Soldat*. The story is a variant of the Faust legend and though the piece was composed toward the end of the Great War (1914-18) its characters and action are not tied to a particular place or time. The choreographer in this recent production brought it up to date with references to America's wars and our state security establishment. In part, she had a rationale: she "decided that the story is really dated." One might think the work not so much dated as "timeless," at least in the sense that it draws us in to a different world where all that is at stake is the bargain with the Devil. In the *New York Times* review[15] of the production one detail caught my attention. The choreographer is quoted as saying, "I couldn't relate to [the story]. I also don't believe in the Devil." So she eliminated the principal character from her ballet.

I do not see much difference between little Tommy's take on *Jaws* and the choreographer's treatment of the Stravinsky work. In her world the Devil does not exist, so there is no place for the Devil in a story.[16]

I am reminded of the Jesuit mathematician and philosopher who served as a sort of prefect in a college dorm. Some students on his corridor asked him if a couple friends visiting from another college could be put up "in that empty room down the hall." The priest said No. Later he explained: if the visitors stayed in that room it would no longer be empty. What a marvelously tidy imaginative world!

In 1899 Henry James returned to England from Italy and wrote: "I crawl, depleted as to purse, wan though bloated as to person, back to my little hole in the sand at Rye [his Sussex home], there to burrow & burrow during an indefinite future."[17]

Here is a biographer's account of that homecoming: "James himself after his long journey was tired, overweight, and worried about money."[18] The novelist's "depleted as to purse, wan though bloated as to person" has become "overweight and worried about money." Strange alchemy, that has turned gold to lead. The review of the biography calls James's journal entry "comic self-depreca-tion." What did the biographer miss? Tone? Irony? Voice? Humor? All of the above.[19]

Is this literalism? The biographer's paraphrase of James's jour-nal entry does miss the point. So much escapes his comprehension but in the interest of what? Perhaps we might speak of a "bottom line" or "Just the facts, ma'am" sensibility, the kind of approach to language expressed in the question "What's the message of your poem (book, symphony . . .)?"

Perhaps I am casting the net too wide. Does every instance of imperceptive reading or hearing or understanding derive from lit-eralism? Or rather, does every such instance derive from a reduc-tionist imagination that cannot begin to grasp nuance, complexity, double entendre? In some cases the person so afflicted has an un-easy awareness that nuance, complexity, and double entendre exist and might be at work in what he or she is reading or hearing, but sees it as a code to be cracked and brought into clear, no-nonsense terms. (Recall the Max Beerbohm cartoon showing Henry James in the witness box and the attorney saying, "Come, come, Sir, I asked you a plain question and I expect a plain answer.")

"Clear, no-nonsense terms": tyrants and autocrats and in fact any-one in charge of anything takes in events and persons and infor-mation according to what fits into their imagined reality, and if it doesn't they can feel threatened. Here is a Stasi officer warning a

writer: "I forbid you to write poems with double meanings! Or poems with triple meanings either! We have experts who can decipher
anything!"[20] The poem, the play, pose a conundrum to the official:
they are subversive of the established order—just how is not clear,
but they are. They are a code to be cracked, a veiled message (as if
a poem has a "message"!), and so experts are on call to decipher
them.

In China, I am told, a traditional means of commenting on state
policy is to use the genre of historical study. During the rule of Mao
Zedong, two Chinese intellectuals wrote about the brave scholars
in the Ming Dynasty (1368-1644) who criticized the emperor and
paid the price for doing so. During the "Cultural Revolution" those
twentieth-century intellectuals themselves paid the price for their
scholarly study of the China of three centuries before, with its veiled
criticism of Mao's despotism. In this case, those who executed the
scholars showed themselves to have some grasp of indirection and
double entendre, though it is probable that nuance was lost on
them. If the Red Guards had been entirely literal-minded, the two
scholars would have survived: "We wrote about events three hundred and fifty years ago," and that would have been that. But the
paranoia typical of tyrants, reductionist and single-entendre as it is,
does bespeak a form of literalism.

The authorized biography[21] of a recent Prime Minister of the United Kingdom offers several examples of this sort of incapacity:

> [The Prime Minister] always had to have double entendres
> explained, and she came to dread uttering them by mistake.
> She saw them as a specifically male thing which would al-
> ways remain a mystery to her. Once she wanted to use the
> word 'blackball' in a speech, and her advisers tried to pre-
> vent her without quite having the courage to tell her why.[22]

> Jonathan Freedland in his review[23] of the biography
> notes that in her makeup

> There was something else missing. [She] was famously
> deficient in humor, needing the jokes in her own speeches
> explained, and Moore sketches a few strokes in a similar
> direction even if he does not stand back and explicitly as-

sess the picture he has painted. He describes [her] "literal-mindedness," how she was perplexed by metaphorical expressions such as "look before you leap."

It may be that a story from her schoolgirl days helps us understand that "something missing."

> [In 1942 in a conversation with a fellow student] she remarked that, really, she didn't think she could believe in angels. 'I have worked it out scientifically that in order to fly, an angel would need a six-foot-long breastbone to bear the weight of its wings.'[24]

It would be unfair to call this "the scientific imagination." Rather, young Margaret Roberts in 1942 imagined that everything could be "worked out scientifically." Science was in service to reductionism.

It is commonly believed that people scientifically inclined tend to shy away from literature and all that, even the liberal arts in general ("loosey-goosey stuff"), and that people comfortable with poetry and novels display great unease with science and its rigorously quantifying procedures. A student years ago told me she was good at math and science but was at a loss when it came to poetry. "I read a poem about a sunset, and then they tell me it's about death. How was I supposed to know that?"

In fact, that supposed opposition in principle of science and imagination is a chimera. Science, together with its cognate or ancillary disciplines, has imagination at its heart. Take, for example, this recent sketch by Freeman Dyson:

> Oppenheimer and Snyder . . . showed that Einstein's theory of general relativity compels any massive star that has exhausted its supply of nuclear fuel to enter a state of permanent free fall. . . . Einstein never imagined and never accepted this consequence of his theory. Oppenheimer imagined it and accepted it.[25]

The scientific imagination sees reality as open to unending investigation, and imagines the results of inquiry as ever-reformable. It is aware of the provisional nature of its hypotheses and theories. What is "settled science" can always be brought into question in the face of new data. Scientists who are self-aware and reflective realize that those data themselves represent what earlier scientists have decided is relevant, according to the paradigm (to use Thomas Kuhn's term) currently regnant. The scientific imagination, therefore, is passionate about inquiry, and inquiry not as "mastering" reality but in humble even reverential service to it. What is more free—liberal—than that open-ended and if I may say so selfless sense of the world and of the inquiring self?

So the young woman's claim to have "worked it out scientifically" suggests that she has missed the point. Her imagination—reductionist, rationalist, procrustean, uncritical—has appropriated a form of thinking that resists being appropriated, and made of it an instrument of smug, adolescent mastery.

All these examples of literal-mindedness in its varieties seem to me to validate the Scholastic principle *Omne quod recipitur secundum modum recipientis recipitur*. Literally, "Everything that is received is received according to the measure of the one receiving," or more loosely, "You get what you get the way you get everything." The image, to the extent there is an image at work in the saying, is of a gallon jar (say) that can only hold a gallon, no more. But not just volume: when we take something in, our very capacities of thinking and feeling come into play. Little Tommy took in the movie as part of his world, and little Otto understood his mother to be talking about actual metal, and young Margaret considered what her catechism told her about angels and, since it didn't fit with reality as she knew it, was dismissive of all angelology. Those examples involve stages of intellectual and imaginative development, but the principle holds for all of us, at any stage, and for anything that crosses our screen. Things fit into our imaginative world, even if they don't, really.

American culture is literal-minded root and branch, so in the course I have used a number of examples where that mindset—the "bottom-line," "just the facts," "no double meanings!" imagination—leads to missing the point. An Ohio State University study[26] revealed that not a few conservatives take the "reporting" and commentary of television's fake-news satirist Stephen Colbert at face value. They think he is one of them.

In a column in the *Washington Post* back in the first months of the Iraq War, Anne Applebaum wrote of an address by the foreign minister of another country that left the Americans present bored and distracted, even though its content was explosive. The official was saying, in effect, that if American foreign policy followed the lines already established, his nation would have no problem with that. It must be remembered that American foreign policy had aroused the conscience of the whole world, that it was seen as brutal and inhumane, involving lies to the American people and slaughter of tens of thousands in Mesopotamia. And here was an official giving the green light.

Why were the Americans, including the press corps, bored? Why uncomprehending? Applebaum explains why

> few of the Americans had really understood the speech. If the foreign minister had stood up, made two jokes, made the one serious point—which was, as I understood it, 'We still support you even if France doesn't'—and then sat down again, the Americans present would have responded with a standing ovation. But in Europe . . . the point of a public speech is not to ruffle feathers, not to offend anyone and not to say anything too directly. Clarity is rude. Obfuscation is a virtue. Americans are different. Americans believe clarity is a virtue and obfuscation is rude.[27]

> The Americans heard the words but did not get the meaning.

Another example of this literalist culture came to me by way of an obituary.[28] R.C. Levin was author of "Report from Iron Mountain," a Vietnam War-era "secret government report." It was a satire warning of the dangers peace would bring. Like the work of the RAND Corporation and the Hudson Institute, Mr. Levin's satire used bureaucratic language and multiple footnotes, and the report in its deadpan style and format could easily be mistaken for authentic. (The Pentagon Papers, released some years later, made Levin's parody seem even more plausible.) Like any good satire (the adjective "Swiftian" comes to mind), the "Report from Iron Mountain" had to be read in a discerning way, which is to say, you had to get the joke. Some didn't, and to this day right-wing anti-government and white supremacist groups (and now, I suppose, some members of the Tea Party) do not get the joke. They take it entirely at face value, and so they adduce it as supporting their conspiracy theories. Disclaimers by Mr. Levin only confirmed their convictions: in protesting that he was the author and that it was a satire of the sort of thing government groups and contractors were doing, he was obviously part of the conspiracy. *Omne quod recipitur*: the people who didn't get the joke lived in an imaginative world where conspiracies abound and where, more basically, double entendre is unknown. Just the facts.

Another *Times* obituary[29] has proved useful. In 1999 the king of the Ashante passed over to the new life after reigning almost thirty years. The obituary sketched his life and something of the culture of Ashante Land (including Ghana). One Ashante commentator is quoted as saying, "The Ashante don't respect you if you speak too literally. In Twi, if you don't know how to speak in parables, you're a nobody." The writer, Michael T. Kaufman, picks up on this, saying, "The king was very much a somebody, and expert in drawing allusions as required."

How unlike our own dear country! I like to think this obituary opened the students to larger worlds. It introduced them to the previously unknown literary genre of obituary. It gave them a glimpse of a different culture, that of Ashante Land. And it offered the possibility of envisioning a world where speaking "too literally" loses you respect.

Finally, in the Old Testament (1 Samuel 18:7-9) there is a wonderful example of literalism. Saul is king of Israel and David his right-hand man. Saul's fortunes are declining while David goes from strength to strength. When they lead Israel's army back from defeating the Philistine forces, women come out dancing and chanting a victory song:

Saul hath slain his thousands,
and David his ten thousands.

Saul is angry at this: the song makes David ten times the war-
rior Saul is!

Saul fixates on the numbers; they take on a life of their own, irrespective of context. And the context is a poetic distich, following
the poetic convention that modern scholars have termed parallelism of members. In this case, the "members" of the poem are words
indicating large numbers, "thousands," "myriads" (there is no real
quantitative difference between the two Hebrew nouns).

If Saul had taken amiss the parallelism of his name and David's
name, that would make some sense: the poetic equivalence (as it
seemed) might suggest that the king's lieutenant was on a par with
the monarch. But no, it is those seemingly unequal numbers that
set him off.

And here we have a clue about literal-mindedness, in the inter-
section of poetry and politics. Saul's jealous, psychologically inse-
cure concern for his primacy renders him incapable of hearing the
"music" of the celebratory chant. His imagination is captive to his
own political—prosaic—concerns.

This chapter is about being literal-minded, living in the land of
single entendre, incapable of "getting" irony, indirection, nuance,
humor: indeed in a real sense incapable of grasping meaning. The
subject requires further treatment.

5

Imagining Others

Let's start with a picture. I saw it in the Washington Post *a couple of years back. I am imagining what is going on with the woman in the photograph. We see her head and shoulders in profile. She is wearing some sort of surgical mask, maybe even a small gas mask. No, the picture was not taken in Beijing or Tokyo; it was taken in Washington D.C., the caption tells us. She was part of a crowd at a rally. The crowd was rallying against immigration. So I imagine she was expressing her view of immigrants, as a threat to public health, unclean, contagious. Filth. That is how I imagine she imagines immigrants.*

"He wants to be the bride at every wedding, the corpse at every funeral, and the baby at every christening." Thus Alice Longworth on her father Theodore Roosevelt. Her description of him certainly accords with his own robust rhetoric and the observations of his contemporaries. My interest in it—apart from its wittiness and applicability to several friends of mine—lies in the realm of the imagination. This girl's mother died shortly after giving birth to her, and she was left in the care of a paternal aunt, and then raised by a stepmother, and frequently shuttled between various households and countries, and never got close to her father. So when she imagined the sort of man he was, it was the public man, the extroverted, larger-than-life man. While surely not the whole story of their relationship, the epigram does capture that person, or persona.

Here is how a successful Hollywood producer is depicted. More precisely, the writer is sketching the producer's self-image.

She seemed to see herself as the ugly duckling at the party, and her every instinct was to inflict the first hurt. She was always ready to erupt with rage and hostility, the reasons for which she is never able to clarify in [the] 573 pages [of her memoir, *You'll Never Eat Lunch in This Town Again*]. . Her style was confrontational, tending invariably to denigration. She was also an injustice collector, who seems never to have forgotten a slight, real or imagined, and she goes out of her way not only to settle scores but to create new bogeypersons. As with all successful fantasts, Ms. Phillips has the gift of keeping the focus on herself. She is never peripheral; in her own mind, in every situation, she is always the sun around which the world as she sees it revolves, spreading not only light but also heat. . . . In the theater of her imagination, Ms. Phillips sees herself as a truthteller, brutally frank to the point of self-destruction, . . .[30]

Another example of imagining someone appeared in print perhaps indecently soon after the subject's death.[31]

[The inventor/entrepreneur] cried a lot. This is one of the salient facts about his subject that [his biographer] reveals, and it is salient not because it shows [the man]'s emotional depth, but because it is an example of his stunted character.

[He] cried when he didn't get his own way. He was a bully, a dissembler, a cheapskate, a deadbeat dad, a manipulator, and sometimes he was very nice. [The biographer] does not shy away from any of this, and the trouble is that [he] comes across as such a repellent man, cruel even to his best friend, . . . derisive of almost everyone, ruthless to people who thought they were his friends, indifferent to his daughters, that the book is often hard to read. Friends and former friends speculate that his bad behavior was a consequence of being put up for adoption at birth. A former girlfriend, who went on to work in the mental health field, thought he had Narcissistic Personality Disorder. . . .

[He] himself dismissed his excesses with a single word: artist. Artists, he seemed to believe, got a pass on bad behavior. [His biographer] seems to think so, too, proving that it is possible to write a hagiography even while exposing the worst in a person.

The reviewer is summarizing the portrait of the inventor she read in the biography, so presumably we are reading how the biographer imagined him. Nonetheless, the excerpt serves as an example of "imagining the other"; and the depiction does seem to present its subject as "other." Not a nice person, as our grandmothers might say.

Almost ten years ago, the NBC television network aired a game show called "Identity," in which contestants were shown various persons and challenged to say, on the basis of their appearance, what they did in life. Unlike "What's My Line?" of the 1950s, the contestants did not get to question the persons appearing before them; they were to make "snap judgments."[32]

Here we might revisit the chapter on assumptions. The snap judgments one makes about persons or groups come from deep-seated images conveyed not—or not only—by personal experience but by the culture one is formed by.[33] To take only the depictions of ethnic groups as commonly used in the United States among members of the historically dominant population, Irish are bellicose drunks (to be hauled off in "Paddy" wagons), Jews are grasping and money-hungry, Blacks are lazy and shiftless . . .

Such perceptions are not limited to these shores. When the United States invaded Iraq, both Germany and France said they would assist in training Iraqi security forces but would not send soldiers, and both called for greater U.N. involvement. People in the U.S., and not only the Bush administration, responded to that offer, the identical offer made by the two nations, in different ways. Germany escaped criticism while France was denounced. As Nina Bernstein writes, "in the American imagination, France is a woman, and Germany is just another guy."[34] Germany exports manly products, BMVs and Mercedes and heavy equipment, France gives the world *parfum* and expensive wines and *haute couture*. The instinctive dismissal of all things French may perhaps be of a piece with more general attitudes toward women in our culture—in "the American imagination."[35]

Here is how a Russian writer depicts his countrymen:

If there is such a thing as the popular Russian mentality, it doesn't like education or diligence, or people with much booklearning. The bookish are often portrayed as Pharisees who have strayed from the sources of life. Tolstoy dreamed of adopting the 'simple life.' . . . I remember how in child-hood my classmates hated people who wore hats on the street even in the spring. They shouted after them, 'Profes-sor!' To this day the words 'doctor of philosophy' and 'pro-fessor' are frequently pronounced in Russian with a jeer: such people are seen as having false knowledge, as being smooth talkers.

Far closer to Russians is the Taoist idea of the superi-ority of muteness to words. Inarticulateness is considered a sign of genuineness. Russian simplicity is coupled with cunning—the primary mental weapon of the commoner. At the foundation of Russian cunning lies a theory of survival which, when coupled with ambition, yields a philosophy of boundless cynicism.

There is nothing more appealing to Russian writers than the idea that truth belongs to 'the people.' This idea surfaces in Pushkin's *Captain's Daughter*. All of Dostoevsky's writing after his imprisonment is imbued with the idea, and Tol-stoy drums it into the readers of *War and Peace*. Radicals and conservatives, revolutionaries and obscurantists alike—all swore by 'the people' and believed in them as in a sacred cow.[36]

From the discovery of the New World, America itself has been depicted in the European imagination in contradictory ways:

Before the American Revolution a school of distinguished Enlightenment philosophers . . . developed the thesis that America was a 'mistake,' its discovery a disaster, its influ-ence a curse to mankind. In its abysmal climate and mias-mic atmosphere plants, animals, human beings, and society degenerated catastrophically, and in Europe it spread dis-ease, inflation, national rivalries, wars, and misery.

This depressing picture was replaced immediately by a new image, formed by the fantasies and hopes of two revolutions, the American and the French, that was in all respects the opposite of the preceding one. 'America' now meant the new-born republic, Europe's temporary utopia, the American Dream. The new image idealized America as uncritically as the old one denigrated it. America was now the best of all possible worlds, a new start and a new hope for mankind, all the Old World debris of kings, courts, bishops, and aristocrats cleared away for a golden age of the present.[37]

Nowadays other images prevail. In the Middle East and throughout much of the world today, the United States is imagined as predatory and calculatedly omnipresent with nefarious intentions masquerading as altruistic efforts. The CIA is everywhere, manipulating everything. (Some say the CIA killed U.S. Ambassador Christopher Stevens at Benghazi.)

Just so, in the American imagination all Arabs are Muslims and vice versa, or something, and all Muslims are suicide bombers eager to restore some empire or other (it's not quite clear which), intent in any case on destroying Western and Christian civilization.

When one imagines "the other" *qua* other, that otherness is the otherness of alienation, where the object of depiction—"them"—is totally unlike "us."

Yet things are not so simple, as the following will suggest. The reporter, Vincent Crapanzano, spent time in South Africa, mostly in Capetown, in the time of apartheid.

The world of the couloured as white South Africans depict it—a world of drinking, fighting, and promiscuity—is a sort of anti-world, contrasting with their own idealized one of gentility, respectability, and, as they say, Victorian morality. It may also refract their own drinking, fighting, and promiscuity or their fantasies of such things. . . . The homelands, in the white view, are filled with witch doctors and sorcerers, the locations are filled with *tsotsis* (thugs) and *skollies* (hooligans) who take on extrahuman proportions...

The distance created by apartheid—apartheid understood not only in legal terms but as a frame of mind—reinforces the predisposition to view the world of the coloureds or, elsewhere, of the blacks as a grotesque anti-world and to act according to that view.[38]

Crapanzano's description of how whites viewed the non-white populations of South Africa makes it clear that the way we imagine others reveals much about ourselves. What he calls "anti-world" cannot be understood except as it shows what lies hidden in the imagination of the ruling minority. As we shall see later, such imaginative depiction gives license to exploit those so depicted. Since imagination creates reality, the way people act toward the imagined other is, in that sense, simply realistic.

6

Imagining the Self

William H. Frist, M.D., when he was leader of the Republicans in the U.S. Senate, published a book called *Good People Beget Good People: A Geneology [sic] of the Frist Family*. It is not listed among the holdings of the Library of Congress, but is available through Amazon. Looking back through the generations of his Tennessee family, Senator Frist saw much to admire: they were all good people.

Clearly this was a deeply held belief he strove to live by, and there is no reason to believe anything but that he was firmly convinced of its truth. As such, it is a useful example, for our purposes, of how people imagine themselves. In this case, the imaginative world embraces forebears and tradition, as well as the satisfaction of knowing oneself to be "good people."[39] (In a later chapter we will meet one person holding a very different conviction about himself.)

I get the impression, from the title of the book, that what Senator Frist thinks (level two) and what is operative in his imagination (level three) are congruent. This is not always the case, to say the least, when people give expression to how they imagine themselves. It often happens that what is at work in what I call level three is not obvious to us ourselves but is obvious to others, sometimes in spectacularly vivid ways. "Thy speech betrayeth thee,"[40] as was said in another context, but "speech" here means how the words reveal underlying images and the affect those images carry.

Here is a fairly straightforward self-description that reveals the imaginative world of the speaker:

If I was 45 and barely walking, you'd see me in one of those church leagues or out there at the parks playing. I just love the game. I used to get in trouble not by stealing or cursing, but because my mom would be at work and I'd be sneaking out to play in a neighborhood park. Anything affiliated with basketball—I was there.

Sometimes, during the stretch of a game, I worry about my competitiveness. My mama called me once and was, like, 'I read your lips and I figured out what you were saying.' And I'm like, 'Aghhh.' Sometimes I might be out there—I'm just being honest—I might say something that I shouldn't say, and then I look over, and there's a little kid looking dead at me. As players, we understand in the heat of the battle you might lose your poise once in a while, but for little kids who look at you as role models, they see you in one light, and all of a sudden you lose it for a split second. Sometimes you say, 'I hope they don't have a different opinion about me.'[41]

The following self-portrait is all too revealing of its author; the "you" is transparently "I."

. . . What starts the process, really, are the laughs, slights and snubs when you are a kid. Sometimes it's because you are poor, or Irish or Jewish or Catholic or ugly or simply that you are skinny. But if you are reasonably intelligent and if your anger is deep enough and strong enough, you learn you can change those attitudes by excellence, personal gut performance, while those who are anything are sitting on their fat butts.

Once you learn that you've got to work harder than anybody else, it becomes a way of life as you move out of the alley and on your way. In your own mind you have nothing to lose, so you take plenty of chances, and if you do your homework many of them pay off. It is then you understand, for the first time, that you really have the advantage because your competitors can't risk what they have already. It's a piece of cake until you get to the top.[42]

For another example of self-revelation, consider the imagery at work in these phrases:

> . . . everyday life, with its painful crudity and hopeless dreariness, . . . the fetters of one's own ever-shifting desires . . . the all-too-narrow realm of swirling personal experience.

". . . painful crudity and hopeless dreariness": the words are abstract—"crudity," "dreariness"—but they evoke pictures of gray, sear, raw landscapes; and "painful" and "hopeless" suggest feelings of depression. Personal desires are confining ("fetters") although, or because, they are "ever-shifting." The feeling of both confinement and impermanence comes out in "the all-too-narrow realm of swirling personal experience."

This is someone who longs for a stable, predictable, safe world that renders personal feelings and desires irrelevant, a reality where one is truly free of all that quotidian, trivial, ephemeral experiential messiness, confining and painful and unpredictable as it is. Happiness would be to live in a realm of abstract, mathematical certitude.

Maybe this is a bad example, since the images the writer's language evokes, such as they are, are far from vivid; but the intensity of feeling they convey seems to me unmistakable. This next statement, though, is fairly concrete:

> Though I don't feel the least bit freakish, I suppose that to even the most understanding, tolerant people . . . I must seem distinctly odd. I keep forgetting that I do very few of the things which constitute conventional living. I don't go to the theatre, movies, concerts, parties. I don't look at television or listen to radio. I have no property or stocks or insurance. I have no family but a niece and nephew I never see and a brother to whom I am as close as to a mild-mannered, short-order cook. I see no friends constantly, only when I'm in their city. . . I have no memorabilia, clippings, reviews, photographs, records, printed or manuscript music. I keep only the letters of one man. I refuse to contemplate the past or the future. I have no plans, no ambitions or infatuations. . . . I assume that the worst is likely to occur at any moment

and therefore celebrate not so much feeling well as not feeling sick. . . . Since I have reduced my needs and interests to a minimum, there will be that much less to die.[43]

I see a spartan apartment, free of all impedimenta save for a box or drawer containing some treasured letters. I imagine the diner and the greeting, "Hello," and the quiet man behind the counter nodding perhaps with a smile; and the writer's brother knowing the same civil, distant relationship. What is the feeling that comes through in this quotation? I imagine serenity, in the stoic renunciation of all the things "most people" surround or divert themselves with, and the acceptance of inevitable death. His death will not matter to most people, in the writer's mind, because most people, for him, likely do not matter. Death will take only him, not his "stuff": he has no "stuff." He has only himself.

Reader, what do you imagine about this man?

Another example, in two stages. Here is how I present the quotation in class:

> When I ask myself why I have always behaved honorably, ready to spare others and to be kind whenever possible, . . . I have no answer.

Students take the statement at face value. Responding to an anonymous homemade questionnaire (Agree Strongly, Agree . . . Disagree Strongly), they indicate that this is a decent fellow, someone they wouldn't mind having a beer with, someone they might feel able to confide in if it came to that.

Then I give them the entire quotation:

> When I ask myself why I have always behaved honorably, ready to spare others and to be kind whenever possible, and why I did not give up being so when I observed that in that way one harms oneself and becomes an anvil because other people are brutal and untrustworthy, then, it is true, I have no answer.[44]

Most students hearing "anvil" think of cartoon mayhem, courtesy of the Acme Corporation, but, that apart, the image is striking. Repeated blows, hammer on iron, and all at the hands of "other people." Other people are brutal: one had better protect oneself. Other people are untrustworthy: keep your distance, you never know what they are up to.

In spite of all, however, the writer chooses to be kind and sparing of others "whenever possible." He imagines himself as a decent, compassionate person surrounded by ungenerous and dangerous people: the only loving person in a brutal world.

I hope that these examples serve to show how one's words reveal one's inner life. Underneath the overt content, and unwittingly informing—and, as we shall now see with more examples sometimes subverting—that content, are powerful feelings and images, and paying attention to that dynamic can be revelatory: from "thinking" (level two) to "imagination" (level three). As in the last example cited, what the writer thinks comes into question from what the writer feels. The following instances will show this tension or (not to put too fine a point on it) contradiction.

As described by Shana Alexander in her 1983 book *Very Much a Lady*, Jean Harris, the headmistress of a prestigious girls' school, who was convicted of murdering her lover, Dr. Herman ("Hi") Tarnower, had an image of herself perhaps not far removed from what her mother sometimes called her as a child, "Miss Infallible": in the murder trial, she spoke throughout of her "integrity." That was her image of herself. She was continually asked about her rival for Dr. Tarnower's affections, a younger woman, Lynne Tryforos, and whether she was jealous of her. Of course given Mrs. Harris's sense of self as a person of integrity, it would have been impossible for her to admit jealousy, or know herself to be jealous. No, she was saddened and dismayed that her lover shared his bed with Lynne Tryforos; but jealous? No.

Under the starchiness of Mrs. Harris's professions, though, and undercutting those professions, powerful feelings seethe, and they come out in powerful language.

Mrs. Harris, what were your feelings concerning the relationship that you knew of between Dr. Tarnower and Mrs. Tryforos?

Actually, I thought it denigrated Hi. . . . I think it depressed me to see Hi be less than I thought he was. . . . But it certainly had nothing to do with my feelings about Hi. I had feelings about myself and my own integrity.

[Were you] at all upset that Dr. Tarnower was seeing Mrs. Tryforos?

Yes, as I said before, I thought it denigrated Hi.

. . . this year on his birthday Dr. Tarnower was planning to be away with Lynne Tryforos. So you were upset about that?

I was sorry. I wasn't upset. . . . Who he slept with was one thing. But this was a man who read Herodotus for fun. This was my picture of Hi.

What did you think of Lynne Tryforos?

I think she denigrated Hi, and she gave me a great deal of trouble with my own integrity.

How did [you] refer to Lynne Tryforos in that last letter to Dr. Tarnower?

Well, let me see. I referred to her as what I had experienced her to be. . . . Dishonest . . . . adulterous . . . a whore.

Didn't you refer to her as your whore? Your psychotic whore? . . . Didn't you use the word slut? . . . Those were very strong terms to use, aren't they?

They are. They are very out of character for me to use. But it's not like me to rub up against people like Lynne Tryforos.

"Out of character." Here are words Mrs. Harris previously used to describe her rival, not in public, not in the courtroom where she is on trial for murder:

vicious, adulterous psychotic
    . . . if that slut comes—indeed I don't care if she pops naked out of a cake with her tits frosted with chocolate.
    thieving slut
    psychotic whore
    self-serving ignorant slut

Tasteless behavior is the only kind Lynn [*sic*] knows—
though to her credit she is clever and devious enough to
hide it at times.

Her voice is vomitous to me

Dishonest, ignorant and tasteless but God knows not
stupid.

On the basis of this language one can call Mrs. Harris self-de-
ceived, but her self-deception is rooted in an unshakeable conviction of her own integrity that shares the same psychic space as her
jealous contempt of that other woman. The imagination works in
powerful but hidden ways.

I offer two more examples of tension or contradiction between level
two and level three. The writer confesses

my natural good will towards all my fellow-creatures, my
ardent love of the great, the true, the beautiful, the just; my
horror of evil of every kind, my utter inability to hate or
injure, or even to think of it; the compassion, the sweet and
lively emotion which I feel at the sight of all that is virtuous,
generous, and amiable.[45]

This lovely self-description is notable for the deep conviction
it expresses of the author's nobility of spirit. Taken by itself, it is
convincing, and betrays nothing that might indicate exaggeration
much less delusion. To assess its veracity, one must consider the
life choices made by the author, and the actions he took. Faced with
the prospect of rearing the child he had fathered with his mistress,
he chose to put the child up for adoption—the same choice he had
made the two previous times he had gotten her pregnant.

Oh why did Providence have me born among men, and
make me of a different species?

I swear to you that of all the Christian virtues none costs me less
than forgiving an injury.

She [his mistress] has been my one consolation in my suffer-
ings, and made me bless them. . . . She has a heart like mine.

Apart from a very few people, I regard [the town of] Môtiers as the most evil and poisonous place one could inhabit.

In his autobiography, his biographer tells us, he looks back on his past sins as the occasional rare failings of an essentially innocent being. That is how he imagined himself. The contrast with the rest of humanity—like the citizens of Môtiers, "evil and poisonous"—is of a piece with that self-image.

One last example is perhaps not much different from the one we just saw. In an encomium to his lifelong companion, this other writer tells us of her extraordinary qualities: "The softness of her laugh was irresistible." "Through her ability to listen, her understanding of the human heart, and her genius for understanding, she was indeed the equal of the greatest who lived."

> But what moved me more than anything were her hands, which never changed. They had been fashioned by work and bore the marks of hard physical labour, yet her touch had a wonderful tenderness which betrayed her heartbreak and helplessness. They were the hands of a poor, wretched old woman who had nothing and no one to turn to yet who found it in her heart to go on giving. I was filled with such sorrow at the suffering engraved on them. I have often wept into these hands and they have often made me weep, though I never told her why. It would cause her pain.[46]

By the writer's account, it is clear that he adored the woman, finding in her "a source of wisdom,   of sure intuition, a bottomless well of continually renewed strength."[47] I am reminded of George Santayana's musings on love:

> [W]here I have added a touch of love, where I have allowed them to bewitch me or to make me suffer, then I was not seeing the reality in them at all, but only aspiration. They may drop out, they may change, they may prove to be the sad opposite of what I thought them: but my image of them in being detached from their accidental persons, will be clarified in itself, will become truer to my profound desire;

and the inspiration of a profound desire, fixed upon some lovely image, is what is called love.[48]

Our writer eventually succeeded in "detaching" his image from his companion's "accidental person" by strangling her to death. In a way inexplicable to him, his professions of undying love were trumped by dark unacknowledged feelings deep in his imagination. He was "not seeing the reality in [her] at all, but only aspiration," aspiration jostling with a kind of resentful loathing that found final expression when his hands tightened around her throat. As for the "lovely image" of her soft, irresistible laugh, "others recall an acid cackle."[49]

So a person can think one way and feel quite another. Where does that leave reason, and us as human beings defined, as we suppose, by rationality?

7

What About Reason?

So convenient a thing it is to be a *reasonable creature*, since it enables one to find or make a reason for everything one has a mind to do.[50]

—Benjamin Franklin

The proposition that we are rational beings has a pedigree going back at least to Aristotle. It embodies a conviction about the human being as self-determining and clear-headed about reality, ever striving for mastery of one's world, capable of controlling, through theory and practice alike, everything from one's "lower" urges and desires to the physical universe itself. Serene, civilized, masterful: rational control creates our essential humanity, only "a little lower than the angels," to quote a phrase from a pre-rational era that still believed in angels.

It follows that each person must be free to assess and choose what is best suited to bring about happiness: after all, our cognitive faculties guarantee that choices will be sensible, well-informed, and well-founded in reality—in a word, rational. John Stuart Mill, for instance, "insists that the individual 'is the person most interested in his own well-being,' and the 'ordinary man or woman has means of knowledge immeasurably surpassing those that can be possessed by any one else.'"[51]

Another thinker from the Age of Enlightenment, however, proleptically cautioned against Mill's rationalistic optimism:

I am far from deprecating that precious gift of God, human reason, or from asserting, that it must always be involved in error and uncertainty. But it is so liable to be blinded by passion, to be warped by prejudices, to be bewildered by the subtleties and contradictions amongst mankind, that it cannot teach with sufficient evidence, or prescribe with sufficient authority the necessary truth and duties now just enumerated. [52]

John Carroll was very much a man of the Enlightenment. Georgetown College (later University) founded by the former Jesuit, Archbishop Carroll, in the 1780s, has been called an Enlightenment school, as opposed to the later Jesuit colleges and universities in North America, whose original purpose was to serve the needs of immigrant Catholics. Still, from the Catholic tradition Carroll had the advantage of a larger view of human nature and human history than was ever dreamt of in the jolly optimism of the Enlightenment. That intellectual movement tended to ignore the power—indeed, the existence—of the imagination.

Now, in our day, there has been a great discovery, or rediscovery. In the realms of psychology and economics and in their derivative fields of endeavor, marketing and politics, the landscape has shifted from when

most psychologists believed that human behavior was primarily guided by conscious thoughts and feelings. Nowadays the majority will readily agree that much of human judgment and behavior is produced with little conscious thought. [53]

In recent years academic psychology has gone through a significant change. Research has shown that "your major life decisions are guided by wants and not beliefs," as Benjamin Nugent put it.[54]

Idiomatic English has always reflected an awareness that the human psyche is far from unitary. We speak of "head and heart," "winning hearts and minds," "change of heart." Is it too much to see in these dualities a spontaneous recognition of what I am calling level two ("thinking," reason) and level three ("imagination")?

To go back no further than the nineteenth century, consider Macaulay. Simon Schama tells us that

[t]o work on the sentiment of the people, to give them ade-
quate understanding of what had held them together or had
pulled them apart, history, wrote Macaulay, needed to be
'received by the imagination as well as the reason. It would
be not merely traced on the mind but branded into it.'

Macaulay's contemporary, John Henry Newman, for all his el-
egance of thought, came back consistently throughout his life to the
imagination. In his 1833 *Arians of the Fourth Century* Newman ac-
counted for the attraction to heresy of certain groups by postulating

a sort of spontaneous feeling that the side of [heresy] was
their natural position; and further, that its spirit, and the
character it created, were congenial to their own.[55]

The spirit that spontaneously felt an attraction to heresy Newman contrasts with a "reverential and sober spirit."[56] A decade later, he wrote that "the heart [!] is commonly reached not through
the reason, but through the imagination." Toward the beginning of
his long old age Newman concluded his *Essay in Aid of a Grammar
of Assent* by stressing how Christianity addresses our minds "both
through intellect and through the imagination," and in a letter of
1872, how "dispositions affect all intellectual processes except the
purely abstract."[57]

From the same century but a rather different thought world,
Richard Wagner reflects the same duality, in his *Opera and Drama*:
"In the Drama, we must become *knowers through the Feeling*. The
Understanding tells us: '*So is it,*'—only when the Feeling has told
us: '*So must it be.*' (emphasis in the original)"[58] In the next chapter,
"Selling," we shall see some ways these realizations come to practi-
cal expression.

Even the dismal science has caught up with the disenchantment
with "rationality," or perhaps better has enlarged its understanding of reason to something less reductionist. The standard model
of economic behavior has until recently taken for granted a kind of
law of "rational expectations," an extension of the hypothesis that

the efficiency of the free market allows predictability about economic decisions, at least on the macroeconomic level.[59]

What brought about a change in the field of economics? Most people would point to the 1974 article[60] of Amos Tversky and Daniel Kahneman and their several follow-up studies[61]—works in the field of psychology, not economics. Erica Goode asserts that Tversky and Kahneman "established, among other things, that losses loom larger than gains, that first impressions shape subsequent judgments, that vivid examples carry more weight in decision making than more abstract—but more accurate—information."[62] Bringing these psychological insights into economic theory called into radical question the idea of the rational actor. The name most associated with this happy wedding of disciplines is Richard Thaler, of the University of Chicago. Behavioral economics, as it is called, contrasts with the work of Thaler's colleagues Milton Friedman and Robert Lucas, the best-known representatives of the "Chicago School" of economics.

The hold that rationality, as commonly understood, has on the minds of academics may be illustrated by a story Kahneman told in a 2002 interview. He was introduced to a famous American philosopher at a party around 1971, and began to tell him about his research. "He listened to me for about 30 seconds, then cut me off abruptly, saying, 'I am not really interested in the psychology of stupidity.'"[63]

In his *Thinking Fast and Slow*, Kahneman describes two "systems" of thinking, System One, System Two. The first

> makes judgments and takes action without waiting for our conscious awareness to catch up with it. . . . System Two is the slow process of forming judgments based on conscious thinking and critical examination of evidence.[64]

I think that Kahneman's System One may well bear a family resemblance to the imagination. In any case, there is a question why the rationalistic and (as I hope we now see) quite unreasonable understanding of reason and rational agency had controlled the thinking of economists. One observer wryly suggested that "there was a 'predisposition' to believe, and ideas "took hold at a deeper level."[65]

That "predisposition" at a "deeper level"—is there a name for that part of the psyche?

8

Selling

Twenty years ago the poet Anthony Hecht taught a class down the hall from where my course met. The course was called "The Catholic Imagination." (What is in this book started to take shape in it.) Hecht would sometimes drop by and ask, whimsically I thought, "How is the Catholic imagination doing?"

Only now do I realize why the whimsy. Twenty years ago that wonderful poet had yet to come to explicit realization about the determinative influence of the imagination. It was only toward the end of his life that he wrote of his growing awareness of

> how deeply personal, quirky and often irrational, are our judgments of taste, . . . residing as these judgments do in some highly private inwardness, deeply severed from what we normally think of as our faculty of judgment.[66]

"Some highly private inwardness, deeply severed from . . . our faculty of judgment." What Hecht describes had long been known to the "mad men," who get paid to sell stuff to Americans. Here are a couple of examples.

A Coca-Cola commercial shown during the Super Bowl years ago introduced Americans to "emotionality." Not that the ad used the word, no. We saw a professional football player, one "Mean Joe Green," hobbling off the field of play to the locker room and being greeted by a young boy, who offered him a bottle of ice-cold Coke. Mean Joe chugged the Coke and hobbled off, and as the boy turned, dejected, away, said, "Hey, kid," and tossed the boy his jersey.

What did a sweaty jersey and an improbable encounter in the tunnel leading to the locker room have to do with selling a soft drink? Emotionality. Viewers were touched by the humanity of this fleeting encounter, and at some level associated that warm feeling with cool Coca-Cola.

A recent ad for Cheerios showed a little girl sitting at breakfast with her mother. The girl asks, "Did Nana ever give you Cheerios when you were a little kid?" The mother nods yes, a little smile playing on her lips as she thinks of her deceased mother. "So," the child says, "when we have Cheerios it's kinda like we're having breakfast with Nana." The mother's face crinkles for a second and she fights tears as gently smiling she nods yes and leans over to give her child a kiss.

Emotionality. At the level of "some highly private inwardness" Cheerios becomes associated with feelings about family and love and innocence and missing a deceased parent and—but why analyze all those associations? The work of the television commercial is done, with the innocent question and the crinkling of the features and the hug. Just like that.

The mind/heart duality, as we saw above, has always been reflected in our language, just as gravity was at work before Newton, but in the last couple of decades it has been the focus of efforts at selling, with millions and millions of dollars at stake. Here is how a veteran advertiser put things:

> You feel the world through your senses, the five senses. And that's what's next. The brands that can move to that emotional level, that can create loyalty beyond reason, are going to be the brands where premium profits lie. . . . There were brands that connected and there were brands that people loved. They *loved* them. . . . a brand that has created loyalty beyond reason, that's infused with mystery, sensuality, intimacy, and that you recognize immediately as having some kind of iconic place in your heart.[67]

"Loyalty beyond reason." Precisely. It is not only economics that has been touched by this recognition of "emotional level" and the place in your heart that is "iconic." We are in the realm where "thinking" is beside the point. I like the formulation quoted from a Hallmark researcher: "It's not that consumers won't tell you what's on their minds. It's that they can't."[68]

Of course, the consumer's affectivity has to be in some way receptive to those brands; the imagination is not a blank slate, and *omne quod recipitur secundum modum recipientis recipitur*. The television viewer has to have feelings about missing a deceased parent, or about human contact (wordless but eloquent); if not, the images and scenarios go amiss. A helpful example of receptivity and non-receptivity comes from the history of Procter & Gamble's magical Febreze®. By the manipulation of molecules this product gets rid of unpleasant smells; it does not mask odors, it eliminates them. Originally it was unscented and originally it sold poorly. Field research revealed why sales were disappointing. The householder with nine cats was simply not interested in using Febreze. Anyone walking into that house from off the street would immediately notice (to the point of gagging) that there was a strong odor of cat in the house, but the householder didn't notice it. In current vernacular, "No thanks, I'm good." Why buy something there's no need for?

What to do? P&G added scent and sales went up. Seems people were amenable to air fresheners. Was it because the whole tricky business of getting them to acknowledge need got bypassed? Who wants to be told their house stinks? The image of Febreze changed. Instead of being something like an intervention, providing relief from a bad situation, it appeals to people as a pleasant finisher, the last step in a good scrubbing or doing a big wash.[69]

Political campaigns, not unlike advertising, are about selling. Appeals to the voters are aimed at the heart, not the head—successful appeals, that is. Almost seven decades ago, this was shown clearly in Robert Penn Warren's novel *All the King's Men*. The narrator explodes in exasperation at the candidate Willie Stark for his pitiably ineffectual rhetoric:

> Nobody would listen to the speeches, including me. They were awful. They were full of facts and figures he had dug up about running the state. . . . Willie knew what was happening, but he didn't know why. . . . He couldn't figure out what was wrong. . . . [Willie] said, 'They didn't seem to be

paying attention much tonight. Not while I was trying to explain about my tax program.' . . .

[The narrator says,] 'You tell 'em too much. Just tell 'em you're gonna soak the fat boys, and forget the rest of the tax stuff. . . . Hell, make 'em cry, make 'em laugh, make 'em think you're their weak erring pal, or make 'em think you're God-Almighty. Or make 'em mad. Even mad at you. Just stir 'em up, it doesn't matter how or why, and they'll love you and come back for more. Pinch 'em in the soft place. . . . Tell 'em anything. But for sweet Jesus' sake don't try to improve their minds.'[70]

Thinking doesn't cut it, "facts and figures" don't work. Go for the "soft place." The man from Saatchi & Saatchi would say "beyond reason." Consumer, voter: people buy, people vote as their imagination has been touched.

The talking heads on television can be heard, and political commentators can be read, using this language. They tell us what successful politicians manage: to speak, not of facts and figures, but of things "that people connect with in a primal way."[71] "Politics is about symbols," said Democratic strategist Steve McMahon.[72] And Mark Danner spells it out:

American electoral politics have less to do with policies than with the manipulation of symbols and with the search to find and artfully present that particular complex of symbols that together most powerfully evoke the emotions desired.[73]

He is talking about the imagination.

In our times, the influence of these realizations on politics has been most clearly evident in the image-making done by White House operatives, starting with President Reagan's adviser Michael Deaver. His successors, arranging backgrounds and lighting for speeches by George W. Bush, went to extraordinary lengths, not just in the meticulous care for every detail but in the dramatic effects they were meant to bring about. At Mount Rushmore President Bush was photographed in profile so that in the picture his face lined up with those of his four presidential predecessors. For a speech in Bucharest, Romania, heavy-duty lights were schlepped across Europe to achieve the proper dramatic effect, the same kind of lights that were trained on the Statue of Liberty as backdrop for Bush's address on the anniversary of the September 11, 2001, attacks. No expense spared, as it seems. And most notably, there was the fighter-plane landing on the deck of the aircraft carrier *USS Abraham Lincoln* on May 1, 2003 to announce the end of major combat in Iraq after the American invasion two months earlier: "Mission Accomplished."

The name most associated with how to target the imagination for purposes of partisan politics is that of Frank Luntz. He is perhaps best known for renaming the estate tax as the "death tax." Spontaneously people reject the very idea of being taxed upon their death, perhaps with images playing of Big Government dancing on their graves. Luntz has put out a few books whose titles may be taken as reflecting the argument I am trying to make: *What Americans Really Want: The Truth About Our Hopes, Dreams, and Fears,*[74] and *Words That Work: It's Not What You Say, It's What People Hear.*[75]

To his credit, Luntz provides his expertise only to conservative causes and candidates (the Republican Party, David Cameron, Silvio Berlusconi), because they represent his political beliefs; he is not a gun for hire. And the G.O.P. has profited from that expertise. Though there are other authors of the party's communication strategies, throughout the first decade of this century the American public's imagination was shaped by the message the Bush-Cheney administration put out. It succeeded in evoking emotions that got voters to reject other views and candidates (there were a few) who espoused those other views. Popular imagination was imbued with "a sense of vulnerability, of loss of control, of looming threat, and of panic and fear," to quote Mark Danner again.[76]

Why did the Republican "messaging" succeed in shaping the public's imagination? Again, we come to the question of the *modus recipientis*. What was the "prior disposition" that made large segments of the population receptive? In a study of John Wayne and the movie genre of the Western, Garry Wills gave us the following:

[The Western] best combines all these mythic ideas about
American exceptionalism—contact with nature, distrust of
government, dignity achieved by performance, skepticism
toward the claims of experts.[77]

Here the emphasis is not so much on "ideas" as on "mythic."
These convictions are age-old, rooted deep in the American imagination.[78] No wonder partisan perspectives got through to people,
on a range of matters from global warming (emended to the more
neutral "climate change") to evolution to immigration to Big Government As The Problem.

What of the other party? Did Democrats learn nothing from
their electoral failures? The short answer might be, "facts and figures" and, therefore, No. The Emory University psychologist Drew
Westen has tried to wake up the Democrats to what Willie Stark
slowly and painfully learned, but they are so in thrall to "reason"
that efforts to get them to take the imagination seriously fail, the
way organ transplants get rejected from a body. Professor Westen
wrote a powerful critique of the rhetoric President Obama and his
party routinely use. He began the piece with (of course) an image
and a story:

It was a blustery day in Washington on Jan. 20, 2009, . . . As
I stood with my 8-year-old daughter, watching the president deliver his inaugural address, I had a feeling of unease.
It wasn't just that the man who could be so eloquent had
seemingly chosen not to be on this auspicious occasion, although that turned out to be a troubling harbinger of things
to come. It was that there was a story that the American
people were waiting to hear—and needed to hear—but he
didn't tell it.[79]

Story! In its adherence to "reason" and "rational" solutions to
carefully analyzed problems, and its touching belief in the "rationality" of the American electorate, the culture of the Democratic
Party pays at best half-hearted attention to the lived lives of people
and their need to hear their own story set forth vividly, humanely.
(Drew Westen would call that need for story "hard-wired" in us by

evolution.) So powerful is the hold "reason" has on the progressive left.[80]

Imagination trumps reason. It is imagination that makes a sometime presidential aspirant able to believe and proclaim that "the Founding Fathers worked tirelessly to put an end to slavery," and know that many will believe her.[81] It is the "rugged individual" imagination that sees our fellow citizens as either makers or takers, and believes that the private sector does things better than government can. It is the way she imagines brown people that put that anti-infection mask on the woman at the anti-immigrant rally.

What are the sources of such determinative images and the "prior disposition" that spontaneously embraces them? And how does all that get changed? That is next.

9

Imagining God

It was the first day of class, a religion class. Before the students could know me and where I was coming from, I gave a quiz, a single question: "If you were to learn with certainty that there is no God, how would you feel?" Almost half the students, seniors in a Catholic high school, expressed relief at the thought. If there is no God, they can be free to relax, they can lead their own lives. Their God was a hostile presence, and freedom was to be out from under his power.[82]

—Rev. William P. Sampson, SJ

Once there was a nun making a retreat (the old-fashioned kind, not a business "retreat") and the person giving her suggestions for prayer—her "guide" or "director"—pointed her to a passage in the Gospels to pray over. It was the one where Jesus tells the story of a shepherd who leaves the ninety-nine sheep of his flock to search for the one lost sheep (Luke 15:4-7).

As we shall see (chapter 13), in the form of retreat devised by St. Ignatius of Loyola in his *Spiritual Exercises*, the imagination is central. So the sister put herself into the story of the good shepherd, and this is how she described the hour of contemplation to her director:

I pictured myself as that lost sheep. It was very vivid. I saw the shepherd seeking me out. He climbed mountains and crossed valleys, fighting his way through briars and brambles, lashed by rain and enduring bitter cold. As I was cowering and shivering he tenderly picked me up and put me

on his shoulders to bring me safely back to the flock, and
then he broke both my legs so I would not run away again.
Do you think she had a positive image of Jesus?

Apparently she was unaware that she was describing a mon-
ster-Jesus. That was how she imagined the Lord, and doesn't everybody?

Job's profession, "Yea though he slay me yet will I praise him,"
comes to mind. Many people simply accept the monster image as
the reality of God, and this acceptance is not infrequently taken
both as orthodox and as central to one's relationship to him. An
elderly man once told me of his daughter's early death (she was
barely thirty) of leukemia. He had lived with the pain of her loss
for decades. He said, "You know, Father, Jesus said 'Suffer the little
children.' Well, my daughter suffered."

Out of respect for his lifelong grief I refrained from explaining
seventeenth-century English usage.

Years ago I discovered that I was on some mailing list because I received a Xeroxed copy of a letter; I was but one of many recipients.
The heading read: "Day of Love." The letter invited the reader to
"picture this heavenly scene." God is sitting on his throne and an
angel reports to him the presence of "a huge crowd waiting to talk
to You." God responds, with a sigh, "What are they asking for this
time?"

How does the author's imagination envision God? Enthroned,
yes: that's biblical. Agents called angels reporting to the Heavenly
Father; check. Human beings making demands on him with their
petitions and needs? Yes. But note the tone of exasperation and even
self-pity in God's response: "What are they asking for this time?" A
pretty grumpy God, if you ask me. That sigh!

The angel goes on: "That's the unusual thing—they aren't asking for anything. They just want to tell you how much they love
You and to thank You for everything."

And how does God respond? His eyes fill with tears as he says,
"AT LAST THEY UNDERSTAND!"

What follows this glimpse of God and his providential care
for humanity is an appeal to designate a certain date as a "Day of

Love." People are to go to church on that day and tell God how much they love him, and not ask for anything—just tell God you love him. "I am striking the match of love; let it spread like wildfire," the letter tells us. "This is going to have a tremendous impact on the heart of God!"

So how is God imagined? Needy, feeling unappreciated and wanting to get some sign people care, only grudgingly responding to human need. Remind you of anybody you know?

Another example of what might be called theological imagination comes from monthly mailings sent to every Catholic priest in the U.S. and Canada. *The Fatima Crusader* is published by a group dedicated to fostering devotion to the Virgin Mary, specifically (as the name of their publication indicates) in terms of her appearances to three children at Fatima, Portugal, in 1917. There, according to the children, she warned of the dangers of modern errors, especially Communism, and of the dire consequences that would befall the Church and the entire world if her warnings were ignored. The flavor of the group's message might be summarized by citing a few headings in their material, both pamphlets and fund-raising letters:

Mercy Has a Time Limit.
Obey or Suffer.
We Need Exorcism Urgently!
Defend the Truth.
Appeasing the Enemy.
The Clear, Near and Present Danger to the Faith.
Deception From Within.
God Will Withdraw Grace.

Enough. The imagination expressed in the materials this movement publishes can be characterized in various ways, but none of them emphasizes God's love. God is impatient, implacable. He is mean. He is "a collector of grievances." The Catholic Church is beset by enemies without and within; betrayals abound, even at the highest levels of ecclesiastical bureaucracy. And God will not allow these things to go on with impunity. He has given fair warning, through the appearances of Mary at Fatima, that failure to obey her explicit instructions (including especially a consecration of Russia to be done publicly by the pope and all the bishops of the world) would lead to apocalyptic reprisals. In the Fatima movement's rhetoric Mary is no less severe than God.

The image of God that comes through is that of a martinet, a strict teacher, a gratuitously cruel official in some Dickensian workhouse, a "hanging judge." This image is not rare in the Catholic Church. God rewards and he punishes, and the touchstone is adherence to Truth, where Truth consists of theological positions taught by the Church through the centuries. (Since this conviction is a-historical, the history and pedigree of a specific teaching never really comes into consideration.)

The late cartoonist Johnny Hart came to embrace Christianity fairly late in life, and the Christianity he embraced was no less exigent than what I have just sketched. His mother had cancer and he prayed for her recovery. After she died of the cancer, he realized that his prayer had been inefficacious, and he reproached himself for letting her die through his inadvertence. What was his mistake? "I didn't ask in the name of Jesus." This technicality in the dynamic of praying was not overlooked by God: Hart's mother died. And that is not all.

His mother was a good person, [Hart] says, but he suspects that she was not a devout enough Christian. He worries that when he arrives in Heaven, she will not be there.

Hart consoles himself with the thought that since "Heaven is a blissful, pain-free eternity," God will erase all memory of his mother—and hence awareness of her absence in heaven—from his consciousness.[83]

Perhaps this severe, ungenerous image of God is a corollary of a more fundamental image of reality in general. Anthony Trollope, in his novel *Linda Tressel*, captures it well:

> Madame Staubach was continually instigating herself to be cruel. . . . Linda [her niece] must be taught not only to acknowledge but in very fact to understand and perceive, that this world is a vale of tears, that its paths are sharp to the feet, and that they who walk through it should walk in mourning and tribulation. What though her young heart should be broken by the lesson . . . ? To Madame Staubach's

mind a broken heart and a contrite spirit were pretty much the same thing.[84]

Are we dealing with a generalized mean-spiritedness overlaid with religious zeal, or has the rigorous asceticism of some forms of Continental Christianity brought about that smug, apodictic treatment of young Linda Tressel at the hands of her aunt? The old theological cliché comes to mind: God created man in his own image and likeness, and man returned the favor. Religious teachings are received according to the measure and mode of the recipient: *secundum modum recipientis*, as we have seen above.

Another, entirely different approach to this question is to try to get rid of images altogether. Certain traditions of mystical experience and teaching have been thought to make this theological move. Strip away all visual or auditory phenomena from God and you have pure mystery, accessible only through a cloud of unknowing. Mainstream theology features some aspects of this approach: Aquinas somewhere says the more we know that we do not know God, the closer we are to the reality of God.

Yet consider what we are left with when we perform this exercise in purification. We are left, willy-nilly, with an image of absence, a vacuum, an empty space punched into the fabric of reality. What does that look like? An accident victim swathed in bandages, unrecognizable? Certainly something inaccessible. The negation of anything imagistic includes also affect and emotion, and there is nothing there but an unreachable, infinitely distant person—except that "personhood" is to be stripped away as well. Anyone who growing up had a cold, distant parent knows the feeling, or feelings: fear, frustration, sense of abandonment and rejection. Anger and resentment.

This exercise in denial of imagination does have one thing in common with standard theological imagining, though: it is never-ending. The classic formulation is, *Deus est semper maior*, God is always greater. But in the project I just sketched, God turns out to be *semper minor*. Nice job!

The point, obviously, is that the imagination can never be bypassed. We are not built that way. Into the image of God as omniscient creeps a fleeting, unbidden memory of that annoying kid in the third grade who had all the answers, or that distant parent you could never share a discovery with because no response of surprise, certainly no delight, was possible. "I have known that from all eternity."

Let me close with another image of God, one that runs counter to all these examples. It comes from Bruce Jay Friedman's 1971 play *Steambath*.[85] The steambath in question turns out to be a transitory state post-mortem, a *purgatorio* set not, like Dante's, in the Antipodes but in New York City. There are various types of characters there, male and female, gay and straight, and a Puerto Rican attendant cleaning, mopping, picking up towels, occasionally speaking into a computer-like device giving instructions about what should happen in the outside world. This is seen through the eyes of a newcomer to the steambath as he takes it all in and gets used to the new surroundings he has just been whisked away to. After back-and-forth with the Puertorriqueño attendant he is told that the attendant is in fact God. Incredulous, he asks, "Why would you be sweeping up, a lowly job like that?" The answer comes: "I like it. It's therapeutic. It's easy on the nerves."

Imagine: a God who picks up after people, doing "a lowly job," because—well, that is what he does. He likes the work.

This of course runs counter to standard images of God, but then so do the images and stories Jesus offers. We call them parables.

10

Parables

Moral obligations are occasionally recommended and com-
mended in [Jesus' life], but no where proved from principles of reason, and by clear deductions, unless allusions,
parables, and comparisons, and promises and threats are
to pass for such. Where [were] all the precepts of this kind,
that are scattered about in the whole new-testament, collected, like the short sentences of antient sages in the memorials
we have of them, and put together in the very words of the
sacred writers, they would compose a very short, as well
as unconnected system of ethics. A system thus collected
from the writings of antient heathen moralists, of Tully, of
Seneca, of Epictetus, and others, would be more full, more
entire, more coherent, and more clearly deduced from un-
questionable principles of knowledge.[86]
—Henry St. John, Viscount Bolingbroke

It is true that Jesus teaches through images and stories, and
nothing more—no theories, no abstract principles. That has not
stopped people from trying to extract from those stories such principles, such generalizations. The story about the Samaritan who
aids the traveler beaten by brigands is domesticated to "Put money
in the poor box." The story about the Prodigal Son is reduced to
"Go to confession frequently."

I have found that when students write of Jesus' use of parables
they routinely describe them as teaching moral lessons by "dress-
ing up" the lessons. To quote from an exam a few years back, "Jesus
was known for placing moral lessons within simple stories."[87]

Students instinctively do this because they have been so taught. If something is intellectually serious, making serious claims on our attention and consideration, it must consist of general principles, expressed in abstract language. Remove the imagistic and narrative garb, you have what Jesus was "trying to get across." In their assumptions about how to read the Gospel parables, students are in continuity with Lord Bolingbroke in his strictures, and with Bolingbroke's disciple Thomas Jefferson, who inscribed the above passage in his scissored-and-pasted recension of the Gospels.

In the next chapter, revisiting literalism, we can go into the kinds and sources of this epistemological Asperger's, but for now it's enough to note how it keeps us from understanding Jesus' parables. I think the best way to understand how parables work is to avoid "principles and deductions" and let a story be a story—two stories, actually.

One story is about King David and the shameful things he did, and the cover-up. (You can read it in 2 Samuel chapter 11.) As always, the cover-up was worse than the original crime, for it involved murder—murder contrived through an abuse of David's royal authority.

The other story involves a prophet, Nathan, to whom it falls to reprove the king for adultery and murder. How would you carry out that mission? Would you speak plainly, "truth to power"? How brave of you. And how inefficacious. How best to get to David? His defenses are powerful. (How do you tell the lady with nine cats that her house stinks? How would the king of the Ashante couch the matter?)

So Nathan tells the king a story.

Two men there were in a certain city;
one was rich and one was poor.
The rich man had flocks and herds, great indeed,
but the poor man had nothing at all
except one little ewe lamb he had gotten.
He nourished her and she grew up
together with him and with his children.
From his morsels she ate;
from his cup she drank;

in his bosom she slept;
she was like his very daughter (2 Samuel 12:2-3).[88]

Sparing his own flocks, the rich man takes the poor man's lamb and makes a meal of it. When he hears this David erupts in anger at "that man," and pronounces him worthy of death. Then Nathan the prophet tells the king, "You are that man."[89]

David was shrewd and skilled in thinking, so by thinking he could easily rationalize his adultery and subsequent murderous cover-up. But a story has a different kind of power. A story draws us in. Listening to it, especially when it involves right and wrong, we spontaneously identify with the one who is in the right and condemn the one who is in the wrong. So, hearing Nathan's tale David's instincts about right and wrong kick in, in spontaneous imagining and, all unknowing, he condemns himself out of his own mouth. That is the power of imagination: "level three" trumps "level two," as this book has been trying to show.

So yes, two things are going on with parables, but they are not some "moral lesson" and its story-line dressing-up, the pill and the sugar that makes it go down easy. It is the story and what the story is about, namely you the listener. It is your story but you don't know it, because it is transmuted into a narrative about someone else somewhere else. It elicits spontaneous reactions, such that you identify with one character and distance yourself from another. It surfaces convictions that you might not be aware of, but that are there, deep down, entwined with images and feelings and radical sense of self. Then it turns toward you and you realize it's a mirror, and that "You are that man."

Here is an example, this time from the Gospels. Jesus tells the story and, again, it is a story about two men. They couldn't be farther apart. One is a member of a religious movement within Judaism in Jesus' time, someone universally admired for uncompromising observance of Torah: he is a Pharisee. The other is a tax collector ("publican" in older translations), universally despised, exploiter of widows and orphans, collaborator with the Roman occupation of the Holy Land: a sinner. Both men go up to the Temple to pray. The righteous man prays a prayer of thanksgiving: he is grateful for going above and beyond in his fidelity to the Law of Moses. The tax collector simply asks that mercy be given him, sinner that he is.

The story draws its listeners in. Jesus' audience would, naturally and spontaneously, identify with the Pharisee and distance themselves from the sinner. They know who is in the right and who is in the wrong. Their spontaneous reaction reveals how they imagine themselves and the world—and God.

Then Jesus delivers the punch line: when they finish their praying and go down from the Temple, it is the tax collector who is "justified" in God's eyes; that is, he the sinner is the one in the right, not the righteous one.

Thus is the world turned upside down. This is bad news for all those who focus on their righteousness. But it is good news for sinners.[90] God loves the sinner. Sinners are the object of his special concern. (God is the attendant who picks up after sloppy, undeserving people. That is his work.)

In his parables Jesus plays off settled images of self and of God. The father welcomes back his ne'er-do-well spendthrift ("prodigal") son, no questions asked. The employer pays everybody the same, irrespective of how many hours they worked. The king opens his banquet hall to everyone, good and bad.

A generous, spendthrift—one might say prodigal—God who is not a calculating, meticulous bookkeeper keeping careful count of good deeds and bad deeds and who is deserving of what.

This image of God is supposed to be good news? It is offensive. So offensive was it to the good people, the "righteous," the religious professionals of Jesus' time that they contrived his execution as a criminal, "a curse of God" (Deuteronomy 21:22-23).

Well, in the way Jesus imagines and depicts God, there should have been no surprise. "My ways are not your ways, says the Lord." "Slow to anger, abounding in love." The God Jesus depicts—the God he imagines—is there in the Scriptures all along, but first the bookkeeper image has to be shattered, and with that shattering also people's (our) sense of self as being in the right, so unlike those awful people over there.

The parables work powerfully to bypass our rational defenses, but there is still that factor I have been calling the *modus recipientis*, what in the listener or reader allows or prevents the parable to do its work. So we have to revisit the form of imagination we call literalism.

11

Literalism Revisited

'But you mustn't fancy,' cried the gentleman, quite elated by coming so happily to his point. 'That's it! You are never to fancy.' 'Fact, fact, fact!' said the gentleman. And 'Fact, fact, fact!' repeated Thomas Gradgrind.

'You are to be in all things regulated and governed,' said the gentleman, 'by fact. We hope to have before long, a board of fact, composed of commissioners of fact, who will force the people to be a people of fact, and of nothing but fact. . . . You must use . . . combinations and modifications (in primary colours) of mathematical figures which are susceptible of proof and demonstration. This is the new discovery. This is fact. This is taste.'[91]

—Charles Dickens, *Hard Times*, ch. 2.

Our students have been taught to prize abstraction and stress principles. They habitually generalize. Their instruction in "critical thinking" has seemingly never included enjoyment or "savoring." At least, this is how the students seem to interpret the "critical" part of that phrase; one wonders if their teachers encourage savoring. Students are in the habit of distancing themselves from what they read, standing apart from it in full analytic mode. (I think of Lord Jim in the lifeboat.)

To counteract this tendency, which their years of schooling seem to have made part of their intellectual DNA, I give an assignment when we study Jesus' parables. It goes: "When Jesus looks at the world around him, he sees . . ." It couldn't be simpler. Read those parables with an eye to what they tell us of Jesus' surroundings and experience of life, his imaginative world. This is an example of what I have in mind:

> [Jesus sees] the homes of the rich ... through the kitchen door . . . hill-country farming done in small patches amid stone fences and briars. . . .There are donkeys, sheep, wolves, and birds; seeds, wheat, and harvests; lilies of the field and fruit trees; patched wineskins and household lamps; children quarreling in the marketplace, and shady merchants, . . . drought and flood . . . the din of war.[92]

The exercise is simple: pay attention to detail, notice, visualize, and (though I don't say this outright) refrain from analyzing or much reflecting. The point is not processing information, but an exercise in imagining. A simple listing or inventory will do nicely. Feel free to savor the pictures you get.

Here is what a student wrote at the end of his paper:

> I must say that as a whole Jesus' view of the world is somewhat oversimplified with regards to emotion and material wealth. My own imagination constructs a world with much more ambiguity than Jesus seems to see.

Two things leap out at me as I read this. "My own imagination constructs a world": this suggests that the student still thinks of imagination as what I call instrumental imagination, as opposed to spontaneous imagining—or maybe it's just that the student means "envisions" but has interiorized the language used in the English department.

The other word that constitutes a tell, at least as I read it, is "oversimplified": "Jesus' view of the world is somewhat oversimplified." Is it fair to hear some dismissiveness here? The student reads Jesus' parables and finds them wanting in sophistication and rigor. Shades of Lord Bolingbroke:

> Moral obligations are . . . no where proved from principles of reason, and by clear deductions, unless allusions, parables, and comparisons . . . are to pass for such.

I am reminded of what Flannery O'Connor wrote to a friend:
I am interested in making up a good case for distortion, as I
am coming to believe it is the only way to make people see.[93]

And Walker Percy's report:

In answer to a question about why she created such bizarre
characters, she replied that for the near-blind you have to
draw very large, simple caricatures.[94]

The self-distancing, analytic intellectual posture is a theme Flannery O'Connor returns to often, associating it with the deracinated
Northerner who lives in a world where everything is a joke. William Barrett reviewing her collected stories shortly after her death
got to the heart of the matter:

The single moral, indeed, that runs through these stories
seems to be that the liberal mind, convinced of its own rationality and self-righteousness, cannot possibly understand
the perverse depths of the than human personality.[95]

("Rationality and self-righteousness": what an interesting
world of speculation Barrett's phrase opens up.)
     I should not make too much of the student's thoughtful com-
parison of his own imagination with that of Jesus. Nevertheless it
appears that he has noted correctly—though not sympathetically—
how the parables show a bias in favor of the poor and a corresponding challenge for the rich.[96] But he has failed to enter imaginatively
into Jesus' world, owing, I believe, to the intellectual habits formed
in him over the years of his education.
     And here we have a means of entry into the phenomenon of
literalism. Education as I understand it gets us used to leaving our
intellectual and imaginative comfort zone and living easily, or at-
tempting to live easily, in other worlds. If we are wedded to—in
fact defined by—the world we call home, and resist the invitation
to that kind of venturesomeness, there is no growth in sympathy or
interior freedom. We are tethered to the views and values we have
grown up with. Those views and values become defining assump-

tions. There is nothing else. Our thinking is univocal, incapable of irony, intellectual playfulness, double entendre. All there is is what we already know. It becomes the *modus recipientis*, the procrustean bed everything has to fit. The word "monism" comes to mind, but let's stay with the adjective "univocal."

Anyway, the purpose of the assignment to "notice" is to make it possible for the students to get out of their own world and into another world, the one revealed in Jesus' parables, and to move easily, in their imaginations, in it. Or not easily—it may well be found off-putting, alien, challenging, frustrating. Either response is a response, and that is part of the point of the exercise.

There might well be resistance to entering into Jesus' world. It is after all "counterintuitive" to the views and values one grows up with in our culture, the way the oracles of the Old Testament prophets Hosea and Amos and Isaiah are. But in our times, as our culture influences the ways we imagine ourselves and reality, the sources of resistance have to do with dominant operative understandings of freedom. Freedom: it was not long ago that "hyperlink" was hailed as the fulfillment of human emancipation. You the reader were in charge. No author would have the final say about how a story turned out. You could move things around as you liked. You were not dependent on the voice of the story-teller: you were the one telling the story. You were in control, and isn't that what makes us human, to be in control?

I see this as an impoverishment, the inability to listen, the reluctance, even resistance, to let oneself be caught up in a story, to be brought out of oneself, "into the dark, where you can't be sure of your footing," to use Flannery O'Connor's image.[97] "Into the dark": terrifying thing, to venture into a different terrain, the previously unknown, and allow space in our imaginative world for something else. Literalism clings to what is familiar and well-known, period. To have something else intruding into that comfortable terrain where we are in charge complicates things, unduly and uncomfortably. How can one be expected to accommodate two different things, not eliminate one or reduce one to other, but leave them each whole in their difference one from the other? Remember the student who was good at math and science but—or perhaps therefore—wrote, "I read a poem about a sunset and they tell me it's about death: how was I supposed to know that?" Sunset or death, one or the other! You can't have both.

That is why, to some, metaphor is such a puzzlement. It's a comparison, fine, but to allow both terms, the thing compared and the comparison, to coexist is intellectually messy and exceeds reasonable expectations of the thinking apparatus. And when a metaphor is brought into a discussion of something, in stand-alone fashion, it seems to this mindset like suddenly changing the subject.[98]

So it is amusing if perhaps predictable to see the best minds puzzled by this thing called metaphor, and seeking to nail it down rationally. Some years ago a Request for Information (RFI) went out from IARPA, a government agency. The acronym (echoing "DARPA") stands for Intelligence Advanced Research Projects Activity.[99]

IARPA, the RFI tells us, had seen that it is important, in carrying out its mission of gathering and interpreting intelligence, to understand metaphor. Research, "especially in the neurosciences and cognitive linguistics, has established metaphorical processes as a fundamental cognitive mechanism that begins in infancy." The "poetic or rhetorical devices" we call metaphors elude the standard methodologies used by social scientists (polling, observation) and so "unconscious views and attitudes are often overlooked or lost," preventing our intelligence services from grasping "contrasts among worldviews." Hence, "IARPA is seeking information about the challenges associated with the science and technologies related to the discovery and analysis of metaphor usage."[100]

Good for IARPA! They are interested in different worldviews, in other cultures and their "views and attitudes," and they realize that pay dirt lies not in the realm of thinking, of theories, of "facts and figures," but in that amorphous and elusive world of "metaphor."

Yet all the apparatus of scientific inquiry, embodying the presuppositions of rational thought, with the precision and comprehensiveness social science methodologies aim at, is brought into play as the sole means of achieving understanding. The questions are asked and the answers sought within that framework: it is not only the *modus recipientis* but the *modus quaerendi*, the mode or measure of inquiry.

Unless the clarity that the inquiry seeks to achieve is recognizable to rationality, the quest will be unavailing. And that way of thinking is itself unfriendly to metaphor. It is either/or, not both/ and. It is univocal, intolerant of ambiguity. ("I forbid you to write poems with double meanings!") The means subvert the end.

What a metaphor!

The "views and values" of rationality crowd out everything else. When we study the Old Testament, for example, students ask, "Did that really happen?" Their assumption is that it is not just a relevant question but the only relevant question. The ultimate logic of this way of thinking dawned on me when I heard the Story Lady on a Christian radio station telling her young audience the parable of Dives and Lazarus (Luke 16:19-31). Jesus' parable tells of a rich man, Dives, and a beggar, and how each fares after death.[101] This is how the Story Lady introduced the parable: "Now children, listen carefully to this story. Jesus tells us about it because it really happened, in his lifetime!"

"It really happened." Did I mention that "Dives and Lazarus" is a *parable*? Yes, of course the story is so vivid that it seems "real." The characters in the parables—the Good Samaritan, the Prodigal Son, the widow seeking justice—take on a life of their own: in our imaginations! But that is not what the Story Lady meant. Though the reality of the parable is imaginative reality, not "factual" reality, the only way she knew to recommend the story to the children listening was to say that "It really happened." Fact, fact, fact!

Want more? Watch the History Channel. Sodom and Gomorrah were destroyed by an asteroid. The Nile ran bloody because of algae. The six days of creation are six geological epochs. The Red Sea parted because a comet happened to swing by just then. If it's in the Bible and the Bible is true, then it all "really happened." Just the way it says—"says" in the way people interpret it of course, but people are not aware of that hermeneutical complexity.

Literalism, then, comes down to a univocal mindset, or imagination, fixated on one thing, hence intolerant of ambiguity.[102] That univocal imagination leads to the reductionist question, "What is the message of your book (poem, symphony, novel)?"[103]

It reads a parable and, impatiently tapping its foot, waits for the disclosure of the "lesson" the story imparts.

More generally, it takes a poem and puts it on the rack until it yields its (singular) meaning. Billy Collins has captured the teacher's amused frustration:

> . . . all they want to do
> is tie the poem to a chair with rope
> and torture a confession out of it.
>
> They begin beating it with a hose
> to find out what it really means.[104]

It reads the creation narrative in Genesis and tries to fit it into what paleontology and astrophysics tell us about cosmic and human origins. Or, finding it to be impossible to match the biblical account to that scientific template, reject Genesis and "religion" as a whole. It is as if Pilate's question, "'Truth'—what is that?" has become "'Truth is an analogous term'—what is that supposed to mean?"

And what would that univocal imagination, with its either/or approach to language and reality make of this:

> [Robert] Frost . . . believed that experience had to be transformed into metaphor in order to make poetry. 'People say, "Why don't you say what you mean?"' he writes in 'Education by Poetry,' a 1931 essay, . . . But in Frost's view, speaking in metaphor—saying one thing in terms of another thing—was not just the principle of poetry; it was at the heart of all speech. 'We like to talk in parables and in hints and in indirections—whether from diffidence or some other instinct.' And he goes even further, suggesting that 'metaphor [is] the whole of thinking.'[105]

A friend who taught eighth- and ninth-grade English for decades told me about the poetry his students have shared with him. They trust him and he would never betray that trust, but in the back of his mind he noticed that their poetry is . . . well, in his words, "There's not a metaphor in sight." They pour out their hearts but those lines of verse are so many journal entries, without more: "My parents have ruined my life." "I could just die." "How can people be so cruel?"

In the univocal imagination there is no playfulness. Everything is all one. Only one voice is heard, because only one voice is at work, and it is the self: there is no other.

W.E.B. DuBois wrote of "double consciousness." In describing the "Souls of Black Folk" (1903), he described, though briefly, the black experience in America. The Negro, he writes, is

> born with a veil, and gifted with second-sight in this Ameri-can world,—a world which yields him no true self-con-sciousness but only lets him see himself through the rev-elation of the other world. It is a peculiar sensation, this double-consciousness, this sense of always looking at one's self through the eyes of others, of measuring one's soul by the tape of a world that looks on in amused contempt and pity. One ever feels his two-ness—an American, a Negro; two souls, two thoughts, two unreconciled strivings . . . . [106]

"Looking at one's self through the eyes of others": that double consciousness works the other way as well. The African-American is well acquainted with those others through whose eyes he looks at himself. In slavery, and under Jim and Jane Crow, and gener-ally in the Land of the Free, in the face of that "amused contempt and pity," historically, if only for the sake of self-preservation he habitually put on a mask of impassivity and deference. But he was fully aware of the attitudes of the majority that set the terms of his existence, and he knew better than to "interiorize" those attitudes. And when he heard the white man saying things like "All men are created equal," that mask of impassivity came in handy. Double consciousness indeed. That the man espousing such sentiments truly believes them only adds to the grim hilarity. Irony abounds, for everyone but "The Man." It is a high price to pay for the devel-opment of a sense of irony, all that oppression and cruel treatment, but it shows in The Man an impoverishment, a spectacular failure, of imagination.

Analogously and in general, it is the poor, the exploited, the oppressed, the powerless who see things clearly; they have that double consciousness. It is the opposite of the univocal, either/or imagination; in significant ways it is a privileged view of the other.

12

Analogy

However reluctantly, then, I feel the remedy to all this cultur-
ally endemic single-mindedness must be brought in, and the reme-
diation involves the "A" word. Read on.

*In metaphoricis locutionibus non oportet attendi similitudines
quantum ad omnia.* (In metaphorical expressions, don't focus
on every single possible point of comparison.)

Thomas Aquinas, *Summa Theologiae*, III q. 8, a. 1, ad 2

A comparison may be very just in its proportions which
does not at all assimilate the things compared.

Anthony Trollope, *Barchester Towers*

After teaching the course on imagination for several years I
came to the realization that our students need instruction in how to
read. However sophisticated their thinking (and it often is), there
is a sinkhole at its center, big as an eighteen-wheeler. They don't
"get" analogy.

But because for them the word "analogy" summons memories
of the SAT, I withheld the word in our class until the grand unveiling toward the end of the semester. Instead, class by class, we
would do an exercise based on a long list of sentences or brief pas-
sages I gave them. The exercise asked the students to do two things.
First task was to explain one of the sentences to the class. The second was to deliberately misconstrue it.

What fun! Except, of course, that sometimes the first explanation was indistinguishable from the second. Here are some examples, from the list.

Katie Couric is the Jackie Robinson of network news.

Both names come from the distant past but enough members of the class had heard of them that general understanding was possible. As Jackie Robinson was the first black man to play (previously all-white) Major League Baseball, so Katie Couric was the first woman to anchor the network evening news.

Now comes the deliberate misunderstanding. "Katie Couric isn't black!" "Jackie Robinson never worked on network news, he was a baseball player!" Jackie Robinson was number 42—is Katie Couric 42 years old? And so on.

What is the source of the misunderstanding? It's too early in the semester to go into all that. So next class meeting we would go on.

From a TV commercial: *Is your six-pack becoming a keg?*

Some students read this as a caution against abuse of alcohol: Are you drinking too much? Out of context that would be plausible, but in fact the TV ad was for a gym: the "six-pack" refers to your flat tummy. Could we say that the first interpretation, besides possibly evincing a sense of guilt about drinking too much, was in a way literalist?

With a fair number of economics and business majors in the class, this 2006 statement from the president of the Federal Reserve Bank in Dallas was a source of merriment:

Despite what you hear from some of the Eeyores in the analytical community, a recession is not visible on the horizon.

Again, this was 2006. Well, he was right about recession; what happened to the economy in 2008 was more than a recession! What did the students make of this statement? Most recognized "Eeyore," and saw that the Fed official was dismissing warnings about the economy as groundless pessimism. Misunderstanding? He is comparing financial analysts to donkeys, stubborn dumb beasts of burden. Or fictitious creatures. Or that they are too short to see what was on the horizon. Or . . .

A few more examples. When the judicial order allowing termination of life support from Terri Schiavo came down, one pro-life spokesman said, *"The judge sent her to the cattle car."*

Few students recognized the image; at most, they construed the statement to mean that the poor woman was being characterized as a cow, a beast. Unless they read widely in twentieth-century history or perhaps had visited the Holocaust Museum here in Washington, the students would not have been familiar with the Nazi transporting of Jews and other victims to work camps or death camps in the East. This example didn't work, owing to a simple lack of information. (The same was true of another example, in which the question during Middle East peace talks, "Where is the Palestinian Mandela?" was met with "Where is the Israeli DeKlerk?" So also of "Dominique-Vivant Denon was Napoleon's Malraux," or "Poggi was the Baron Haussmann of Florence." Those references are too obscure, to the students, to be helpful.)

Try another. *Lennie Briscoe's been known to kick the ball onto the fairway.*

This was said by Assistant District Attorney Jack McCoy about veteran detective Briscoe in an episode of the long-running television drama *Law and Order*. A little communal thought revealed that the image comes from golf. When the ball goes into the rough, according to the rules the player hits it out; that's one stroke if the player is good and/or lucky; multiple strokes, with the score mounting up, if he's not. Someone willing to violate the rules will make sure no one is looking and "kick the ball onto the fairway" instead of hitting it. The detective has the reputation of bending the rules of police procedure. What would be the misunderstanding? Lennie is a bad golfer. (Or the D.A. has, unaccountably, changed the subject.)

The late television sports reporter Jim McKay covered the Olympics for it seemed countless Olympiads, and when he approached retirement, this is what Tony Kornheiser said of him: *At 80, Jim McKay can't throw nine innings any more, but he still has a fast ball.*

Since no one in the class had heard of Jim McKay everyone assumed he was a superannuated pitcher, but once the TV and Olympics connection was explained, it all became clear: Jim McKay was being *compared to* a pitcher. He had lost some stamina but still excelled at what he did. In this instance, the misconstrual of the sentence preceded the correct understanding.

Carolyn Hax in her syndicated column gave this advice: *"Now it's going to take multiple, mutual apologies: your sister for overstepping her bounds, and your girlfriend, for holding out for her half of the baby."*

Virtually no one got this. Almost everyone assumed the case

presented to Carolyn involved some question of paternity or cus-
tody of a child. But a few students who knew their Bible recognized the story in 1 Kings (chapter 3) of the two women disputing
before King Solomon. Once that was cleared up, the point of the
allusion emerged. One of the parties in the dispute Carolyn was
giving advice about was being selfish and, very likely, standing on
"principle" unreasonably, and an apology was in order. That is the
point of the comparison. But one misconstrual was especially rich:
Carolyn Hax sees herself as King Solomon!

In retrospect I think the exercise might have been pedagogically
more useful had I asked the students to go through a kind of plod-
ding explanation, to "unpack" the metaphors. Take things step by
step. Keep it simple. Line up the two sets of terms and images next
to each other.

Thus, Jackie Robinson was the first black man to play major
league baseball and in being first opened the way for others to fol-
low. Katie Couric was the first woman to anchor, solo, the evening
network news. Jackie Robinson and Katie Couric were each first in
their respective positions. That is the point of comparison.

Jim McKay despite advanced age was still good at his job, the
way a skilled pitcher is good at his job. That is the point of the comparison.

"Six-pack" and "keg" are metaphorical for flat stomach and pot
belly. Don't let yourself go; stay trim. That is the point of the comparison.

Some financial analysts are like Eeyore the donkey friend of
Winnie the Pooh, unreasonably, chronically pessimistic. That is the
point of the comparison.

The judge's decision to remove life-support systems from Terri
Schiavo, in the view of a commentator, was like the consignment
of Jews to death camps in the Holocaust. That is the point of the
comparison.

What is the source of misunderstanding of these metaphors (for
all allusions are metaphorical)? Look at the quotations at the head
of this chapter, from Aquinas and Trollope. Focus on the point of
the comparison and don't get distracted by the particulars of each
term. As Trollope tells us, the comparison may "not at all assimilate the things compared"; misunderstandings come from "focus-

ing on" (Aquinas) the terms of the comparison in every respect, in their details. Look rather to the "proportions" of the comparison, that is, its point, narrow and limited as it is.

(None of what I have said should be taken to deny that allusions and other analogies carry with them important aspects of the other term of the comparison. For example, as I write, sabers are rattling in Eastern Europe and Russia seems to be eyeing its neighbor to the west, Ukraine. So far I've not heard the word *Anschlu✶*. But if someone did use it, would it be fair to see it not just as a historical reference to Germany's annexation of Austria in March of 1938 but as implicitly likening Putin to Hitler? I think it would be fair, and intended, so long as the point is Hitler's expansionist adventurism. Allusions and analogies in general are evocative of what something is compared to. Misunderstanding occurs when one or another aspect of that term of the comparison is made its central point, and the central point — Putin's land grab in Crimea is like Hitler's in Austria and later in the Sudetenland — is missed or obscured.)

Two more examples of misunderstanding, of the many that abound in our times. The first comes from an interview with the TV political commentator Chris Matthews.[107] He told the interviewer, Mark Leibovich, that he aspired to be identified with the upcoming political campaign, to put his impress upon it. Can we think of bullfighting, he asked, without thinking of Hemingway.

Stop here. What is the point of the comparison, its "proportions"? Surely it is the identification, in the public's mind, of a person — in this case, a commentator — with something. To spell out the proportions: As Hemingway was identified, in the public's mind, with the "sport" of bullfighting, so Chris Matthews wished to be identified, in the public's mind, with the current political campaign.

Misunderstandings? Are you comparing politics to bullfighting? Are you comparing yourself to Ernest Hemingway?

In fact, it was the latter question that Mark Leibovich asked. Matthews did not take it well.

Another example, showing the same kind of confusion. The historian Doris Kearns Goodwin explained the factors that led to Al Gore's loss in the 2000 presidential race. One factor was the candidate's reluctance to call on his predecessor's help in campaigning for him. Kearns Goodwin adduced a historical precedent. Forty years before, Richard Nixon was reluctant to have his predecessor campaign for him, and he lost too. That was the point of the comparison.

Here are her words:

> In the 2000 election, Gore didn't use Bill Clinton. It's the same mistake Nixon made in 1960. Nixon didn't let President Eisenhower, who was much respected and loved by the American people, campaign for him until it was too late.
>
> Can you guess what was made of that? Yes, a commentator 'assimilated the things compared,' ignoring the 'proportions' of the comparison. So what came out of Rush Limbaugh's mouth was *'Bill Clinton respected and loved?!!'*[108]

The grand unveiling: Dear students, this whole long exercise, class by class, was meant to get you familiar with the complexity and yet simplicity of comparisons, and the confusions they are prey to. I hope by now you are familiar and comfortable with the way these things work. So next time you hear someone on TV erupt in outrage that. "You're saying he's another Hitler!" or "How dare you compare that to the Holocaust!" remember these lessons and realize that those talking heads have missed the point. They allowed themselves to be distracted by the details of one or another term of comparison, ignoring its "proportions." AND the word, the shorthand term, for this way of comparing things or persons or events to other events or persons or things is—*drumroll*—analogy.

Alas, besides the sloppiness in "getting" analogies there is the habit of mind that simply fails to see similarities in persons, events, or things, a kind of incuriosity, an "atomistic" imagination that takes things as separate items, without more. During the 2012 presidential campaign after we had noted some of the language and images used about President Obama I played the clip from *Blazing Saddles* where the new sheriff rides into town (as in chapter 9, above). I assumed —imagined—that the class would immediately see how Mel Brooks's depiction of American racial instincts was being played out in our politics four decades later.

It didn't work. No one got it. How foolish of me, to forget that things need to be explained, and that it is just good pedagogy to get the students talking to see what they make of what they just saw, and to "connect the dots" for them if need be—as need there was. One doesn't want to insult their intelligence, but that is a risk teachers have to take.

Incapacity to understand analogy is at the heart of literalism. The un-analogical imagination can nevertheless be reached. Nathan's story got to David (blindsiding him), and though Jesus' parables work slowly they work like time bombs. Even the literalist imagination can be transformed. In some circles that experience is called conversion. I am calling it re-imagining. How does it come about? When it works, it works, but sometimes it doesn't. What makes the difference?

13

Re-Imagining

I see Assumptions and Literalism as twin means of understanding the faculty we call imagination.

Assumptions reveal how we spontaneously imagine—grasp, understand, envision, depict, represent—reality, including our selves. As mentioned earlier, we are not even aware of our assumptions until they are brought to our attention and, sometimes, called into question; and then our reaction (puzzlement, disorientation) reveals our tacit, deep-down conviction that we are not making assumptions at all, or if we are that our assumptions are unassailable. Puzzlement and disorientation show that we are no longer in our comfort zone. "But I always thought . . ." or "But I've always been told . . ." or, my favorite, "You've got to be kidding."

Literalism is similarly revelatory. I wrote above that for the literalist there is but one voice. There is no "double consciousness," no irony, no humor. There is only the self. But this is not simple, naked solipsism. The self is tightly identified with something, so tightly that it is all-defining of the self. Of course, all of us find our identity in something or someone, and that can change as we go through life. The teenager dies her hair black and wears chains over her black biker jacket, and then after some years is still wearing black, but now it is your basic black dress with pearls. We change, and the look that gives expression to our self changes. When asked why we no longer do such and such, we answer, "That's not me," or "That's not me, it never really was." Examples of this self-identification would fill a book much longer than this one.

Consider the case, though, of someone who is so totally identified with a job, a cause, a party, an ideology, a race, a nation (and so on), that there is no space between self and the job or cause or ideology espoused. When the defining object is another person we speak of obsession or at least infatuation, and it is creepily uncomfortable for the object of desire.[109] When the object so totally invested in is a cause or ideology, we call it fanaticism.

How to tell the difference between simple identification with something and such total, slavish, un-self-critical fanaticism? Try making a joke about the cause. You will get "That's not funny!"

We are back to the *modus recipientis*. Exclusive, intense embrace of the sort I have been laboring to describe has been called fundamentalism. It determines all one's perceptions and actions. It swallows up everything that does not fit with it. There is no point of entry to allow second thoughts or critical reflection, for such level-two intellectual activity is beside the point and is easily eluded: different viewpoints are received as arrant error or as gross irrelevancies or indeed as blasphemy.

So: we have seen that literal-mindedness can be the result of several factors, along a spectrum of factors, starting with neurological impairment (the stroke survivors of chapter 1). Incomplete neurological development (those frontal lobes) accounts for the self-absorption and incapacity for self-humor so salient in teenagers. It often shows itself in simple incuriosity, a lack of interest in anyone or anything outside oneself. "Lack of interest" understates the condition. One is unaware that there is anything or anyone to be interested in or have one's curiosity piqued by. Just try to get through to someone caught in that condition; you will get "Whatever." This is a stage the human being goes through (in our modern Western culture anyway). In some cases this incuriosity takes the form of a principled, a deep-down resistance to leaving the comfort zone of oneself and one's familiar world. Although it is a stage, some never get past it, alas.

Spilling over from adolescence into what ideally is maturity, comes the far end of the spectrum where the self is swallowed up in obsession or fanaticism.

So there are these twin identifiers of the self. The way words and images reveal the way one's imagination is shaped (chapter 6), assumptions and literalism more generally bring to light the imaginative world one inhabits and the deep-down convictions one lives by. Assumptions and literalism provide powerful defenses against the interventions of reason. "Facts and figures," unless they accord with the reality one's imagination has established as settled, are unavailing.

There is, I believe, a way to get through these defenses, a doorway as it were. It is possible to affect the *modus recipientis*. As we saw in the chapter on parables, the imagination can get around defenses and draw one into another world, another reality. The term often used is "re-imagining."

But here we must make an important distinction, one that goes back to (what we saw in chapter 2) instrumental as opposed to spontaneous imagining. When people speak of re-imagining, as in many television commercials for products and services, they refer to tinkering with established products and services. When they speak of thinking "outside the box," the thinking is still defined by the box. This is the imagination as providing a fix to problems: instrumental.

Here a couple of stories will be useful. The first is about a wonderful educational experience that was just good teaching.

"Adopt a Disability Day" was a great success the one time it was held on our campus.[110] Students had raised money to rent wheelchairs and other equipment so that anyone who wished to take part—for the day, for an hour—could adopt a disability. Headphones blocked out all sound, so if you wore them you became deaf for the hour or the day. (There are ways to simulate blindness, but they involve many and daunting difficulties, so that possibility was not offered.) Using a wheelchair gave you a new experience of getting around campus. It isn't easy, what with hills and sidewalks. A campus you knew well was suddenly unfamiliar. You had to think ahead, working out alternate routes to class or dorm. The routes were inevitably roundabout and complicated, and time-consuming: you had to leave plenty of time to get from here to there.

I think the term "kinesthetic image" is used for this kind of experience. I used a wheelchair to get to class and back, and for the entire class period. I couldn't go to the blackboard and write on it, because I couldn't get up from the chair. I got a new appreciation for how people who are physically challenged experience life. What to me was new, that instinct of always plotting a route ahead and figuring out how long it would take, is to them a given, a second nature. Before that day I never imagined it. It was a good exercise, entering into the lived experience of so many people I had previously seen only from the outside, as it were.[111]

I just wrote "them." I don't think of them as "them" any more. It was not reading books or even watching movies that gave me that appreciation and what I believe is understanding-from-within. It was sharing life as people in wheelchairs experience it. Absent the chance afforded by "Adopt a Disability Day" to have that experience, the next best thing is probably stories about what it is like, told by those who know it. If we who hear the stories are receptive (*omne quod recipitur* etc.) our imagination might be engaged, and our imaginative world enlarged.[112]

Not a few students declined to take part in the disability simulation. Presumably they were not receptive. Why might there be resistance to venturing on such an experience or even hearing stories about disability? An unwillingness to face disturbing or unpleasant realities? A theodicy that sees affliction as divine punishment? Self-absorption? Breaking into a settled reality—a comfort zone, a set of convictions, a desire to stay with one's security—any or all of these.[113]

Such breaking-in is a kind of violence. "That really shook me up." "I don't know how to process that." "Let me go off and think about that." Re-imagining can be as painful as it is liberating.

The second story was serviceable in my previous book[114] and may be so here as well. As it was told to me, the story is about a priest carrying on a peripatetic ministry in Appalachia and a family he visits who live in the hill country. (Cue scenes from Walker Evans's Depression-era photographs in *Let Us Now Praise Famous Men*.) The priest noted how the family would fetch water from a stream down the "holler" some distance away, and noted also that outside their house there was a well. Hearing this story in class the students have the same reaction you do now, reading it: Why didn't they draw water from the well in their yard? Thinking plus a little imagination yields several possibilities. The well is dry. The well has water but the water is brackish. The children might fall down the well, so it stays covered.

These reactions are sensible, reasonable. They represent an exercise of what I am calling instrumental imagination; the "re-imag-ining" is a tinkering with a problem.

Why not use the well? "Rope's too short."

We are still in the realm of "using the imagination," i.e., instru-mental imagining. A problem is noted, and a fix for the problem comes to mind. The visitor, the outsider, sees clearly what the fam-ily fails to see, noting what he deems a failure of imagination. He buys a longer rope! The family are delighted. It saves them that trip to fetch water several times each day.

Months later the priest returns and finds them again fetching water from the stream down the holler. Why? The answer: "Rope broke."

Now we are in the realm of spontaneous imagination. The fam-ily lives in a familiar, given, settled reality: the way things are, and always have been. That is how they see things. That is the reality their imagination accepts and, in accepting, creates. We speak of the culture of poverty, with its hopelessness and passive resigna-tion, but that way of seeing things misses the point. The point is that the conditions of life and sense of a future that are associated with poverty are all there is. That is their imaginative world. That is them, period.

Now we, outsiders that we are, spontaneously imagine another reality for that family. From our experience of life, spontaneously we react with compassion or exasperation or a combination of the two, if compassion and eye-rolling can be combined. I like to invite the students to consider that the story of the Appalachian family and the well-not-used and being locked into a fixed way of seeing things is a parable. "You are that man." You are that family. (Did you assume otherwise?)

There are stories and there are stories. Some we read or hear, and we can be caught up in them. Some others catch us up in our very lives, as participants (say, using a wheelchair), and those espe-cially can be transforming.

In The Netherlands Protestants and Catholics lived in separate worlds. There was no love lost between the two. Each saw the other as "other." Then the German army rolled in. During the Nazi occu-pation a resistance formed, and it included Protestants and Catho-lics. They were working together against a common foe, in a common cause. That effort, day by day and month after month, formed close ties. Antipathies and ignorance vanished. Assumptions were left behind. Newly formed, deep sympathies freed them from the comfort zone of assured convictions. Growth in a sense of possibilities about the other rendered the other no longer alien. Each religious group re-imagined the other religious group. This de facto ecumenism redefined their whole imaginative world.

Another story. Picture this:

> In the first week of September 2001 [in North Belfast] ,. . . little girls were walking up the road to the Holy Cross school, hand in hand with their mothers or fathers. From behind a human screen of policemen in riot gear, grown-ups were spitting, throwing bottles, and screaming abuse: 'whores,' 'sluts,' 'Fenian bastards,' 'animals,' and the chant, rising in pitch and menace, of 'scum, scum, scum.' The little girls were Catholics. The adults screaming at them were Protestant residents of the enclave in which the school is situated. . . . In the struggle between rational politics and visceral, historically rooted ethnic hatreds, it seemed all too clear that there could be only one winner.[115]

"Visceral": This is level-three imagination. Given the weight of history, going back to the seventeenth century, and historically charged resentments, what could bring neighbors to re-imagine one another? A common enemy perhaps, but there was none, since for the Protestants the British presence protected them and Catholics saw the British as enforcing the status quo of repression. In the case of North Belfast, what made the difference was a political process, with give and take, skillful negotiation, restoration of local governance, and above all deep feelings and vivid images of Irish identity. All the political processes made sense only in light of that commonly held—if differently understood—value. Fintan O'Toole puts it this way:

> . . . the decision of the governments [of Great Britain and the Republic of Ireland] to engage them in argument and negotiation broke down precisely that self-protective barrier that

Joseph O'Neill identifies so well: the self-righteous conviction that they could not have been doing harm to the very
entity that they held so dear: the Irish people. This conviction thrived on repression, but could not survive the kind of
reflection that anyone involved in a political process must
engage in.[116]

I ended chapter 5 with a quotation from Vincent Crapanzano's
series of articles on apartheid-era South Africa. Here is the rest of
the passage:

It is perhaps no accident that several English and Afrikan-
er office workers with whom I spoke agreed that they had
come close to colored colleagues only after some violent argument in which each side said what it thought of the other.
Violence, at some level, may be the only way to break out of
the circle—to enter into a relationship rather than to depict
and exploit.[117]

We speak of "clearing the air." Those level-three images and
emotions that shape our reality can come out in full force (sometimes surprising us ourselves), not in measured, rational disclosure
but geyser-like. Those powerful feelings and unlovely images reveal the truth about ourselves, and when the other person gives
way to the same kind of emesis there is, finally, the possibility of
mutual understanding and even affection. Pretense is left behind.
We are finally taking the other person seriously, as they are. Now
that is re-imagining.

14

Re-Imagining God

This book comes out of courses I have taught at Georgetown University, and at Georgetown's campus in Qatar, over the past three decades. The courses are called "The Catholic Imagination" and "The Apocalyptic Imagination in Christianity and Islam." They are Theology courses, so it will be fitting to end this book with some theological perspectives, especially since I hope those perspectives will serve to pull together themes treated in the first fourteen chapters.

For example, the sometimes vexed question of belief and faith and the difference if any between them can be seen in light of level-two and level-three operations of the mind. Beliefs are a matter of thinking. They are subject to rational examination; they admit of correction upon reflection; they change in the face of new data and fresh perspectives. When we say "I believe," that profession is an instance of "thinking," but what validates or grounds it are the convictions lying deep in the imagination, not the imagination as instrumental but as spontaneous. I think those convictions embody "faith."

As we saw in chapter 6, beliefs about ourselves do not necessarily accord with the reality of ourselves. There is a disconnect. To review:

The man who describes himself as kind and honorable, "ready to forgive whenever possible," deep down imagines other people as "brutal and untrustworthy." His self-image is rooted in contempt for others. He, in contrast, is a loving person—the only such one in a world full of despicable people.

We read, from another writer, confessions like this self-description: "my natural good will towards all my fellow-creatures, ... my utter inability to hate or injure, or even to think of it." This disarming profession of his own purity and nobility of spirit come from a man whose imaginative world had no room for the children his mistress bore him, or for his mistress except as "she has a heart like mine." In this case, his beliefs about himself are fully in accord with his deepest and most firmly held convictions. It is the appallingly narcissistic choices he made that call into question the reliability of his beliefs and the faith they reflect.

The headmistress found guilty of murder truly believed she was not jealous of her rival, and her belief was rooted in her unshakeable conviction about her "integrity." That was her faith, seemingly, to the day she died. She never realized the depth of jealousy and vindictiveness her "integrity" masked, even when confronted with her own self-indicting words.

The student (in our Introduction) who was impervious to evidence, resistant to "facts and figures," unknowingly revealed his conviction that he is a Good Student. That conviction, the faith, the operative creed he lived by, defines him as who he is, sad to say.

So it cannot infrequently happen that the belief we profess is at odds with our true convictions, our faith. "Thy will be done" coexists with a kicking and screaming rebelliousness against God. There is a brief prayer Catholics are taught to say: "Sacred Heart of Jesus, I place my trust in Thee." A friend of mine came up with the formula, "Sacred Heart of Jesus, I do *not* place my trust in Thee." Thus belief is made consonant with faith—a faith that in this witty formulation is given expression as what it is. Call it unfaith. It is the imagination of an unbeliever. Yet this sort of unbeliever spontaneously chooses to be honest and to stand before God in nakedness of spirit, without pious trappings or self-induced proofs of righteousness. Rather like that tax collector (the "publican") in Jesus' parable, if you think about it.

We have seen that the ways we imagine ourselves and present ourselves to the world can trigger a sense of irony in others. In looking at the modern Roman Catholic Church, no less a theologian than Harvey Cox has called attention to one of its salient characteristics, how though historically it has firmly opposed "the acids of modernity" the Church has taken in "one of the most corrosive" of those acids: "literalism." Here, again, the Church's belief about itself has been undermined by an operative faith, interiorized from the over-whelmingly literalist culture of the West of the last few centuries. (The joke goes: Apologetics is pouring hot lead into the hole where the enemy was last sighted.) We become what we hate.

Cox writes:

> Not only the fundamentalists but also their mirror image, [certain biblical scholars and theologians], have forgotten the essentially mythic and symbolic quality of religious language. It is as though one of the most unattractive com-ponents of modernity has taken its revenge on religion by seeping like some invisible but lethal vapor into the inner sanctum of the churches themselves. [For Pentecostals and charismatics] language, including religious language in its present debased state, is suffocating faith. . . . It is not for nothing that thoughtful observers of worship have detect-ed a surprising similarity among silent Quaker worship, speaking in tongues, and the Latin Mass.[118]

One of the questions put to a newly appointed bishop at his in-duction ceremony gets him on the record as swearing to preserve in its integrity "the deposit of faith." The teaching function of a bishop is taken (or reduced) to consist of upholding Truth, as "Truth" is identified with doctrinal formulations of earlier centuries and re-cent papal pronouncements. As this ideal shapes the imagination, or reinforces an imagination already so shaped, it leads to wariness and vigilant suspicion and an inquisitorial cast of mind about any-thing that looks new. What is new is dangerous, subversive of the faith and morals ecclesiastical authority is sworn to safeguard. It is an easy progression from this form of imagination to the leaden, or wooden, language of the current vernacular liturgy. Literalism is risk-averse.

In the last chapter I tried to show that reconciliation is a matter of re-imagining the enemy, the other, through experience, through story. This is a dangerous project. There is no assurance that con-flict will not grow greater, especially since as Vincent Crapanzano wrote, "Violence, at some level, may be the only way to break out of the circle [of projection and mutual incomprehension]—to enter into a relationship rather than to depict and exploit."

Re-imagining has to start with oneself, of course. Recall the Pharisee in the parable: "I thank you God that I am not like other men." Given this cast of mind, why would such a person be willing to re-imagine himself and run the risk of overturning an identity labored at and honed and polished over a lifetime?

We are back at the Febreze conundrum. We are so used to what others detect as unpleasant odors that we do not even notice them, so we see no point in buying a product that makes them vanish. How can something vanish if it doesn't exist? How can a spiritual need be remedied if there is no awareness of it?

In the introductory material to his handbook of re-imagining, the *Spiritual Exercises*, St. Ignatius of Loyola sets forth a principle that, if put into practice, can go a long way toward taking care of the problem.[119] It calls for hermeneutical generosity, but makes no claim apart from a kind of "What if?" Consider the possibility that you might not have all the answers. What if what your neighbor is saying might be right, or at least not as wrong as it seems to you. Ignatius urges one to be prepared to put a positive interpretation on what the neighbor is saying. This provides a point of insertion into a process of listening and dialogue, breaking out of a circle (to use Crapanzano's term) that encloses one inside one's imaginative world.

The attitude thus counseled as a presupposition for going through the Spiritual Exercises can be applied throughout one's life, but in the context of a retreat it comes down to a willingness to lend one's imagination to what God is wanting to do in and through the retreat.

For imagination is at the heart of Ignatius's Spiritual Exercises. Divided roughly into the four weeks of a thirty-day retreat, the process Ignatius suggests brings in the imagination from the very beginning. Thus, in considering the shape of one's life and choices and the pattern of choices that makes that life what it is, one exercise would have the retreatant imagine herself on her deathbed reviewing her own life. How does it look, now, at its end? The natural reaction of course would be "If only!" Regret, even compunction,[120] come out of that imaginative experience of honest looking at wrong turns taken and possibilities foreclosed (Hopkins: "Our ruins of wrecked past purpose"). That deathbed relativizing of one's history allows an experience of freedom, leaving behind rationalizations and self-excusation.

What one experiences in week one of the thirty-day retreat can lead to a salutary sense of oneself in full honesty about one's life choices, relationships, actions. In my experience of making and directing Ignatian retreats, the result can be a giddy relief at the fruits of honesty: no longer having to sustain a favorable self-image. Ignatius puts it strongly. Seeing oneself for what one is, imagining oneself as viewed by a host of onlookers, Ignatius writes,[121] in the astonished sight of all creation, the angels, the saints, the heavens, sun, moon, stars, the elements, fruits, birds, fish and animals—the whole array of reality—one is moved to marvel that the earth has not opened to swallow one up. *Con crecido afecto*, Ignatius writes: that realization is shot through with strong, spontaneous emotion. How different is this image of oneself from that of the eighteenth-century savant quoted above ("My natural good will toward all my fellow creatures").

I spoke of lending one's imagination to God in the retreat. The realization of one's own spiritual need, because it is centered in the imagination and therefore bypasses our rational defenses, is a vivid, powerful experience but (perhaps surprisingly) in no way depressing. It is accompanied not only with the relief just mentioned but even with what Ignatius calls consolation. It is God lifting the veil, leading us to the heart of things, sharing with us his knowledge of us. And God's knowledge of us is inseparable from his love of us, in our need.

The Exercises then take us into the Gospel narratives about Christ (ministry, passion and death, risen life), and here again the imagination is key. Ignatius would have the retreatant put herself or himself into the scene *con la vista imaginativa*. For example, in contemplating the Nativity he suggests taking on the role of a servant in the stable.[122]

And not only *la vista*: Ignatius uses what he calls the application of the senses. Return to a scene already imagined and go through it again, this time with the audio turned off (so to speak)—just the picture. Again, with only sound track (so to speak), no picture. And so on, through the five senses. Savor the scenes imagined. At the end, as always, dialogue with God about what you have experienced in this imagining.

Many have a problem with this way of proceeding. They are given to thinking! That is why silence and solitude are crucial elements of an Ignatian retreat. After a few days you settle in to a "holy nescience," as the expression is. The buzzing of ordinary consciousness (level one) fades, and you become attentive to your surroundings—trees, birds, stars at night, the very air you breathe.

Many have another problem: imagining itself. Some retreatants "use" their imaginations, manufacturing the Gospel scenes and the characters in them, as if they are Cecil B. DeMille or Franco Zeffirelli (or Mel Gibson!) making a movie in their minds. (Remember the exercise in our chapter 2, where I tried to show the difference between instrumental and spontaneous imagining.) This effortful manufacturing of images is wearisome, because it is artificial.

But if the retreat's silence and solitude and sleeping and daydreaming and lack of distractions work their magic, imagining a scene and putting oneself into it can be effective, revelatory of deep feelings and long-hidden memories. Once the imagination is freed, ordinary consciousness gets out of the way and surprises erupt. In the first directed retreat[123] I made, forty years ago, Luke 7:36-52 was suggested as a scene to be contemplated in imagination. That is the story where the woman reputed to be a sinner bathes Jesus' feet with her tears, giving grave offense to the righteous Pharisees looking on. In the subsequent conference with my retreat director there was this exchange:

HE: How did it go?
ME: Pretty well. I found it easy to get into the scene.
HE: Who were you in that scene?
ME: Well, a Pharisee of course!
HE: What did Jesus say to you?
ME: Um, nothing. See, I was sort of at the edge of the crowd; but I could see everything that was happening; it was very vivid.
HE: Did Jesus look at you?

ME: Um, no, see there was a pillar blocking my view of
him, except of course his feet as the woman washed
them.

HE: So in your imagination you spent the greater part of
an hour in the same room as Jesus and there was abso-
lutely no interaction between you? What do you think
that might mean?

He was pointing out what was not just a failure of imagination
on my part, but one that revealed let us say a certain self-distancing
from Jesus. It came as a great surprise to me, but it was only through
the imagination that that revelation of the state of my soul came.

As the years went by, that same retreat director worked out
a way to get retreatants to relax into imagining a Gospel scene. This
is what he would suggest:

Enter your imagination. It is early morning. You are in a
room alone. The Apostles and close followers of Jesus are
scattered into four or five houses for the night. There are
two or three others in the same house with you, each in a
separate room. You are waking up in this strange room.

Get into the senses, the feel of things, the shapes, colors,
and sounds of early morning. Let your present mood sur-
face, especially any negative elements—a reluctance to be at
prayer, for example, or a worry about after the retreat.

You usually say a psalm on rising. There's a knock on
the door. A disciple who is your friend: 'Let's get coffee.'
You go to the kitchen. Already there, is one disciple with
whom you have great difficulty. There is a typical friction.
At the worst possible moment for you, Jesus enters looking
for coffee. Others come in gradually.

When all are present Jesus announces that he will
preach today on a certain hillside. You all head out in twos
and threes, getting out the word to different parts of town.

You arrive at the hillside and sit down with one or two
disciples. Jesus is about to start.

Now read a sentence from the text suggested. Read it
a few times, then close your eyes and imagine the voice of
Jesus. Hear him—not just the words, but his voice.

Make sure you remain realistic in your imagining—always people around you, friends and others, even as he preaches the parable. Take it slowly.

If you cannot get started, do not pray for help. Rather, give your imagination something easy to imagine: a child wanders into the room and you must take care of it. Spend 2 or 3 minutes helping the child before returning to the material. It could be a dog, or a cat, or a cousin of yours. Peter comes to you. 'Your cousin is here.'

During this time, do no reflecting. Don't try applying the mystery to your life. Don't try to figure out possible meanings. Rather, be listening to voices with their peculiarities, and their emotions. Be seeing faces and expressions, be feeling the weather, tasting food.[124]

Notice in these directions the emphasis on the senses, in the context of early-morning quiet and being alone; how gradually one imagines others entering the scene (perhaps experienced as intrusion into a peaceful experience, perhaps experienced as welcome relief from loneliness); how tendencies to "think" are gently set aside; and the indispensable encounter with "a disciple with whom you have great difficulty" in the imagined experience. "You have great difficulty": sometimes the term "charity problem" is used.[125]

Notice also how in this method of contemplating a Gospel scene, starting slow, with no feeling of urgency to get on with it, the retreatant is given full scope for imagining. The only expectation is that someone (but who?—it often comes as a surprise) will knock at the door, and that eventually, in an almost leisurely way, there will be a get-together with fellow disciples, and that one of them will be a "charity problem," and that Jesus will enter the scene. All in good time. Rushing things is as bad as thinking about the meaning of it all.

That encounter with the person you dislike is central to the exercise, for two reasons. Nothing gets the imagination active like running into someone who drives you crazy, or who routinely treats you unfairly, or . . . Imagining that other person with all her or his annoying mannerisms and thoughtlessness and self-importance is so easy to do, it's impossible to be distracted. It really gets the juices flowing, as they say.

The other reason is that love of enemy is central to the gospel. First, though, you have to acknowledge that you have an enemy: you have to face up to it. And, that established, you have to face the person. The person has to be real, not just notionally but in the depths of your being, in your imagination. And that facing-up has to be in the presence of Christ. Sometimes a retreatant will appeal to Jesus in the imagined scene for support in the argument, or turn on him in anger: "That's right, take her side!" The imagination is a realm where things long hidden come to light, with no thought of what "should" be. What "should" be is a kumbaya world where God's in his heaven and all is well, serene and consoling and not particularly challenging to us. In contrast, God is found in the deepest part of us, the imagination, when in our imagination we are led to an encounter with our "charity problem," our enemy. The face of God cannot be seen except as it takes the form of that other person.

Crapanzano recounts the experience of apartheid-generated division and how "at some level, violence may be the only way to enter into a relationship rather than to depict and exploit." In his Spiritual Exercises, St. Ignatius gives us a forum where that violence can be experienced and full honesty be safely attained and expressed. The imagination at work in this way can be the means through which a new self and a new world and a new experience of God are shaped and created. For "the kingdom of God suffers violence," and whether in an office setting in Capetown or in the safety zone of a retreat, "the violent bear it away."[126]

15

Implications

The Spiritual Exercises can cut through complacent ignorance of and disdain for the other: we become aware of the stench of our many cats. But, in the Exercises, through exercises of imagination, what might make a violent entry instead gently yet still disturbingly gets through to the retreatant. It is disruptive and therefore does entail a certain violence affecting one's tidy imaginative world, precisely by the interaction with the enemy but always, imaginatively, in the presence of Christ. The violence is contained, so to speak.

I must say, knowing the dynamics this book has tried to lay out has helped me understand certain things I read or hear or even experience myself. I am coming to a fuller and perhaps habitual realization that what people say or do can represent beliefs coming from level-three convictions, and that in the face of such visceral, deeply rooted convictions it is beside the point to take words and actions on the level of "thinking."[127] Engaging them on that level is "wasted breath." Facts and figures make no matter. Outrage is misplaced.

Even so, when I hear politicians and pundits spouting irrationality, I feel a nagging desire to set them straight. Where does that instinct come from? On the "Physician, heal thyself" principle, I realize it must represent something deep in the way I imagine others and myself (chapters 5 and 6). The Village Explainer, the Omniscient Corrector surrounded by irrationality? Very plausible.

Here is an example of what at first hearing provokes outrage, and is impervious to rational "correction." Recently we heard a Nevada rancher sharing his thoughts:

I want to tell you one more thing I know about the Negro. [I drove by a Las Vegas housing project and] in front of that government house the door was usually open and the older people and the kids—and there is always at least a half a dozen people sitting on the porch—they didn't have nothing to do. They didn't have nothing for their kids to do. They didn't have nothing for their young girls to do. And because they were basically on government subsidy, so now what do they do? They abort their young children, they put their young men in jail, because they never learned how to pick cotton. And I've often wondered, are they better off as slaves, picking cotton and having a family life and doing things, or are they better off under government subsidy? They didn't get no more freedom. They got less freedom.

These perceptions are both enraging and innocent. Mr. Bundy is speaking from the heart. No experience, no story have ever impinged on the way he imagines African-Americans and African-American experience, history, lives, humanity. His anthropological disquisition is "innocent" because he is simply, without self-consciousness or self-protectiveness, describing the world of experience he has imagined. And of course there is no one at his elbow to nudge him toward caution in speaking. (His acolytes live in that same imaginative world.) The anti-world of apartheid we have seen earlier is precisely that: an anti-world. Bundy's imagined "Negro" world is not an anti-world. Except for the standard image of Us (hard-working, deserving) and Them (lazy, unproductive), there is in his depiction no projection of some hidden self. He might as well be describing an exhibit he saw in Disneyland.

So it is a mistake to hear expressions of such level-three convictions, such "faith," as if they are the result of rational thought. Hear them for what they are. The battle is with principalities and powers, not flesh and blood. Still, I can't help wondering what remedies there might be for effecting a conversion, a transformation of that imagination. Are we trapped in the ways our imagination has been shaped? Sounds like determinism!

The way to liberate the imagination is—the imagination. As we saw above, it's the imagination re-imagining. It comes about in a number of ways. Immersion into another world of experience is one. Lord Macaulay wrote of foreign travel:

> [One] is transported into a new state of society. He sees new fashions. He hears new modes of expression. His mind is enlarged by contemplating the wide diversities of laws, of morals, and of manners.

He cautioned, however, that such immersion into another world, of itself, might well change nothing:

> But men may travel far, and return with minds as contracted as if they had never stirred from their own market-town.[128]

Macaulay is underlining the *modus* that determines how the new sights and sounds of foreign travel get, or don't get, to the traveler. The imagination can be tenacious, resistant and even impervious to what is new; so "immersion" is not a sure-fire remedy for prejudice. It has to be immersion that includes personal investment of the sort we saw with the wartime collaboration of Protestants and Catholics in the Netherlands, or "Adopt a Disability" Day, or the love of country that transcends confessional differences (as in Northern Ireland), or even the eruption Crapanzano describes. Observers on the sidelines remain unaffected.

With the Spiritual Exercises, the personal investment comes from that initial step of entering the retreat and sticking with it, generously or maybe tentatively lending one's imagination to the process, or rather lending the imagination to God as he is at work in the process.

Then there is story. Parables work like time bombs, as I suggested. As with immersion and travel, we are led out of our own world into another world, the world of the parable, and later, *Boom*, that moment comes when we hear, "You are that man."

A common, and indispensable, element of the experience that brings about re-imagining is that at the heart of the new world that we discover, and in discovering discover ourselves, is the enemy — the other: unknown, or if known then known only as part of an anti-world.

Interreligious dialogue is an activity that pulls one off the sidelines onto an existential field of play. As with the Spiritual Exercises, there is the initial commitment to a process where you don't know where it will go and how it might end up. But it is an involvement, and that is the point. People involved in interreligious—and, analogously, ecumenical—dialogue know that the point of the dialogue is not to celebrate what we all have in common but what are our differences.[129] Even when that is granted and we undertake to go on and confront those differences, there lurk within each of us those level-three mostly unexamined because unknown images of the others in the dialogue: a whole new level of difference. My Hindu friend might well take for granted, like the air he breathes, the caste system, which has been called "perhaps the greatest single evil in the modern world," relegating vast numbers of human beings to a demeaning and hopeless fate [130] Shall I pretend? Should I bring it up as something to dialogue about? Let sleeping dogs lie?

My evangelical partner in dialogue might well feel, deep down, what a woman in Belfast confided to a documentarian's camera: "Well, Catholics practice idolatry, don't they?" Catholics worship bread. In consuming the bread and wine of Holy Communion they show themselves to be cannibalistic. Does my friend imagine he is sitting across from some moral monster?

And so on. Everyone in that dialogue contains images of the others, rooted in lessons—stories!—absorbed in childhood, reinforced in sermons, wrapped in memories of atrocities, persecutions, pogroms, spoliations, humiliations. Should those feelings of grievance and instincts for recrimination be brought to the table? What if they remain undetectable, and all the more powerful for being so?

In the interreligious dialogue I have taken part in, some of this was at least adumbrated by consideration of "obstacles to dialogue." Most of all, though, it was the friendships formed over the years of meeting that made it possible to go on in the dialogue. It was not a side-stepping of prejudices but a new consciousness forged that rendered them moot. "Amor vincit Omnia," so to speak.

In a sense, we were living up to the ideal St. Ignatius holds out in number 22 of the Spiritual Exercises, the famous Presupposition. Again and again we had the opportunity to hear and interpret in a benevolent spirit what others were saying. We were friends.

Ignatius's presupposition itself is rooted in another, older, and deeper formulation. Ignatius urges openness to what the other person is saying or teaching or (presumably) doing. That openness is of the sort we freely bring to conversations with our friends. We are glad to hear them out. We want to clear up any possible misunderstanding, to assist them if we can in sharpening their insights or gently correcting what strikes us as being amiss in what they say.

Ignatius is counseling the same instinct of generosity in all our dealings with others, especially others with whom we differ. As I read it, his counsel is not simply to avoid the self-indulgence of playing Gotcha! It is to befriend that other person.

What is that called, that befriending of someone who stands for what is alien or perhaps abhorrent to you? Befriending someone who could conceivably be called your opponent, your adversary? The short form is, "loving your enemy."

Often among people who are seriously religious or "spiritual" a phrase from the Sermon on the Mount is heard: "Be ye perfect." More helpful, though more challenging, is the fuller form: "Be ye perfect, as your heavenly Father is perfect." What is often lost sight of, however, is that the context for this one-liner is what Jesus has been saying about that heavenly Father:

> But I say to you, love your enemies and pray for those who persecute you, that you may become children of your Father in heaven, because he makes his sun rise upon wicked people and good people, and brings rain upon just people and unjust people. For if you love those who love you, what payoff do you have?
>
> Don't tax collectors do the same?
>
> And if you greet only your brethren, what are you doing over and above?
>
> Don't the gentiles do the same?
>
> Therefore, you be perfect as your heavenly Father is perfect.[131]

The whole point is that God is not a "respecter of persons": he treats all the same, because he loves all. So the "perfection" Jesus mandates, by which we share in God's being, consists in loving the enemy.

This love command is absolute: no ifs ands or buts. It breaks in to our settled world. It pokes at sleeping dogs. It mocks our pious professions. It clears away the elaborate structures we erect to shore up antipathies and assure us of our rectitude. It makes a violent entry, but is put sweetly, sensibly, in almost cost/benefit terms.

What are the inducements to take that love command to heart? "To heart": it can transform the imagination, that level-three center of our knowing and loving, the very *modus* that determines what we see and hear. We are talking about conversion. Very likely we have known people who have been converted from something to something else. Does the transformation last? Very often, no—like the man in the Epistle of James who sees his reflection in a mirror and then wanders off unchanged.[132] Only a radical transformation of the imagination can be effective as a conversion.

That kind of conversion helps us take things in stride when others do not "behave." That's easy when we love them.

But the chief "payoff" is that we share in God's life. If you believe Jesus, what makes God God is that he is entirely focused on us in our need, our lovelessness. He is self-forgetful: love means that we go out from ourselves to the other. Same with God. Here we could fast-forward to First Corinthians 13:5, "Love does not seek what is its own." Jesus is in effect promising that that interior freedom will be ours.

That instinct of course will not occupy our consciousness. Love is self-forgetful. If anything, our focus will be on the ways we do *not* love our neighbor and *a fortiori* our enemy. By definition our habit of loving will be hidden from us. It is the Febreze phenomenon in reverse: we don't notice the sweet fragrance of God's working in us.

Notes

1   Cf. Georgetown University Dean of the College of Arts and Sciences, Dr. Chester Gillis, at the Georgetown College Faculty Convocation address on January 22, 2013: "In an article published this month at *MailOnline.com*, psychologist Jean Twenge reports on data compiled over four decades that indicates a dramatic rise in the number of students who describe themselves as being 'above average' in areas of academic ability, drive to achieve, mathematical ability, and self-confidence. Researchers also found a disconnect between the students' opinions of themselves and actual ability. Objective test scores show that their writing abilities are far less than those of their 1960s counterparts. The author also notes that there has been an increase in anxiety and depression."

2   C. Thomas Gualtieri, MD. *Brain Injury and Mental Retardation: Psychopharmacology and Neuropsychiatry* (Philadelphia: Lippincott Williams & Wilkins, 2002), 145.

3   Chris Gayomali, "This Pill Could Give Your Brain the Learning Power of a 7-year-old," http://theweek.com/article/index/254721/this-pill-could-give-your-brain-the-learning-powers-of-a-7-year-old

4   Kurt Andersen, "Commentary: The Metaphor Zone," *Studio 360*. June 11, 2005. http://www.studio360.org/story/107015-commentary-the-metaphor-zone/.

5   Søren Kierkegaard, *Training in Christianity* (Princeton, N.J.: Princeton University Press, 1944), 185.

6   J. H. Elliott, "Américainerie," *The New York Review of Books*, January 22, 1976. http://www.nybooks.com/articles/archives/1976/jan/22/americainerie/

7   The range of imaginative possibilities has increased over these last decades: now, students might imagine the surgeon as the boy's "other father," his father's male partner or spouse. The point remains the same, however.

8   John D. Early, *Maya and Catholic Cultures in Crisis* (Gainesville: University Press of Florida, 2012), 251-252.

9   Cf. John J. O'Callaghan, "Teaching 'ex Cathedra' as seen from the classroom," *America*, December 28, 1996.

10   Jonathan Mirsky, "An American Century in Asia," review of Michael H. Hunt and Steven I. Levine, *Arc of Empire: America's Wars in Asia from the Philippines to Vietnam; The New York Review of Books* June 20, 2013.

11   "A Narrative of the Voyage to Maryland, fall of 1633-March 1634," in Robert Emmett Curran (ed.), *American Jesuit Spirituality: The Maryland Tradition, 1634-1900* (NewYork: Paulist, 1988), 54.

12   Norman Cantor, *In the Wake of the Plague: The Black Death and the World It Made*, cited by Eamon Duffy, "On the Brink of Oblivion," *The New York Review of Books* May 23, 2002.

13   H. Allen Orr, "A Mission to Convert," *The New York Review of Books*, January 11, 2007.

14   Tony Kornheiser, "Girls and Guise," *The Washington Post,* October 9, 1994.

15   Daniel J. Wakin, "Stravinsky's Devil, Reignited," *The New York Times*, June 5, 2011.

16   The same impoverishment of imagination can be seen in Rush Limbaugh's reaction to the movie *Babe* (1995). He stopped watching after fifteen minutes or so, because "pigs can't talk."

17   Henry James, letter to Howard Sturgis, in Sheldon M. Novick, *Henry James: The Mature Master* (New York, Random House, 2007), 299.

18   Alan Hollinghurst, "Passion and Henry James," review of Sheldon M. Novick, *Henry James: The Mature Master; The New York Review of Books*, February 14, 2008.

19   In January 2006, John Tierney of *The New York Times* wrote, in a piece called "Male Pride and Female Prejudice," "It's still a universal truth, as Jane Austen wrote, that a man with a fortune has good marriage prospects."

20   Quoted by Alessandro Barchiesi, *The Poet and the Prince: Ovid and Augustan Discourse*, and cited in the review by Bernard Knox, "Playboy of the Roman World," *The New York Review of Books* January 15, 1998.

21   Charles Moore, *Margaret Thatcher* (New York: Knopf, 2013).

22   Ibid., 388.

23   "The Unknown Maggie," *The New York Review of Books* September 26, 2013.

24   Moore, Ibid., 33.

25   Freeman Dyson, "Oppenheimer: The Shape of Genius," review of Ray Monk, *Robert Oppenheimer: A Life Inside the Center; The New York Review of Books* August 15, 2013

26   Heather L. LaMarre, Kristen D. Landreville, and Michael A. Beam, "The Irony of Satire Political Ideology and the Motivation to See What You Want to See in The Colbert Report," *The International Journal of Press/Politics,* April 2009, vol. 14, no. 2. 212-231.

27   Anne Applebaum, "A Failure to Communicate," *The Washington Post* October 8, 2003.

28   John Kifner, "L. C. Levin, Writer of Satire of Government Plot, Dies at 82," *The New York Times* January 30, 1999.

29   Michael T. Kaufman, "Otumfuo Opoku Ware II, King of the Ashante, Is Dead [sic] at 79," *The New York Times* March 14, 1999.

30   John Gregory Dunne, "A Star Is Born," review of Julia Phillips, *You'll Never Eat Lunch in This Town Again, The New York Review of Books,* May 16, 1991.

31   Sue Halpern, "Who Was Steve Jobs?" review of Walter Isaacson, *Steve Jobs, The New York Review of Books,* January 12, 2012. Jobs' self-description as artist reminds me of G.K. Chesterton's comment, "There are many real tragedies of the artistic temperament, tragedies of vanity or violence or fear. But the great tragedy of the artistic temperament is that it cannot produce any art."

32   Alessandra Stanley, "To Tell the Truth, What's Their Line?," *The New York Times,* December 18, 2006.

33   See Colin Woodard, "Up in Arms," *The Tufts Magazine,* Fall, 2013. "It isn't that residents of one or another nation all think the same, but rather that they are all embedded within a cultural framework of deep-seated preferences and attitudes—each of which a person may like or hate, but has to deal with nonetheless." http://www.tufts.edu/alumni/magazine/fall2013/features/up-in-arms.html#sthash.DodNRQKm.dpuf

34   Nina Bernstein, "For Americans, It's French Sissies Versus German He-Men," The New York Times September 28, 2003.

35   Ibid.

36   Viktor Erofeyev, "The Possessed," review of Edvard Radzinsky, *The Rasputin File, The New York Review of Books* March 29, 2001.

37   C. Vann Woodward, "Spaghetti West," review of Ray Allen Billington, *Land of Savagery, Land of Promise, The New York Review of Books,* June 11, 1981.

38   Vincent Crapanzano, "A Reporter at Large: Waiting," *The New Yorker,* March 18, 1985. Note that Crapanzano, like any good field reporter, is using the categories of the host country. Under apartheid the categories used the term "Coloureds" for those of mixed race, "Blacks" for other non-whites up-country. For purposes of racial classification Asians were categorized as Whites.

39   Al Kamen, "Sen. Frists's 'Good People,'" *The Washington Post*, January 28, 2004. Mr. Kamen tells us that "the catchy little phrase, 'Good People Beget Good People,' is a saying passed down from Frist's father in a letter in 1997, when he was 89 and nearing death, to his great-grandchildren, setting out his views on life. Actually, we've heard this often at club teas on Sunday afternoons."

40   Editor's note. Fr. Walsh did not footnote this. It seems to be Matthew 26:73, which the King James Version renders as "Thy speech bewrayeth thee." The meaning is the same.

41   Antawn Jamison, *The Washington Post*, May 8, 2005. Jamison played forward for the Washington Wizards among other teams (ed).

42   From an obituary of Richard M. Nixon, *The New York Times*, April 24, 1994, quoting a 1979 interview that appeared in The *Washington Post*.

43   Editor's note. Although Fr. Walsh did not append a citation to this excerpt, it is from a letter written by American composer Alec Wilder. See Whitney Balliett, *American Singers: Twenty-Seven Portraits in Song* (University Press of Mississippi, 1991), 19.

44   Sigmund Freud, letter to James J. Putnam, July 8, 1915, *Letters of Sigmund Freud*, ed. Ernst L. Freud, translated by Tania Stern and James Stern (New York: Basic Books, 1960), 308.

45   Cited by Maurice Cranston, *The Solitary Self* (Chicago: University of Chicago Press, 1997), 182. Note also Cranston's comment on p. 199: "Christ was not seen by him as the redeemer, not even as the object of adoration and prayer. Christ was rather a being in whom he saw himself prefigured, a good man ill used, a victim of society's hostility."

46   George Steiner, "Stranglehold," review of Louis Althusser, *The Future Lasts Forever, The New Yorker*, February 21, 1994.

47   Ernest Becker, *The Denial of Death* (New York: Free Press/Simon & Schuster, 1973), 168.

48   George Sardayana, *The Last Puritan* (New York: Charles Scribner's Sons, 1936), 580.

49   George Steiner, op. cit.

50   Benjamin Franklin, *Autobiography* (ed. P. Conn; Philadelphia: University of Pennsylvania Press, 2005), 31. Emphasis in Franklin's text.

51   Cass R. Sunstein, "It's For Your Own Good!", review of Sarah Conly, *Against Autonomy: Justifying Coercive Paternalism, The New York Review of Books*, March 7, 2013.

52   Archbishop John Carroll, in Robert Emmett Curran (ed.), *American Jesuit Spirituality: The Maryland Tradition, 1634-1900* (New York: Paulist, 1988), 139.

53   Leonard Mlodinow, "Most of Us Are Biased, After All," review of Mahzarin R. Banaji and Anthony G. Greenwald, *Blindspot: Hidden Biases*

of Good People, The New York Review of Books, April 4, 2013. *Blindspot* is one of several studies published in recent years, including Max H. Bazerman, Ann E. Tenbrunsel, *Blind Spots: Why We Fail to Do What's Right and What to Do About It* and Nassim Nicholas Taleb, *Fooled by Randomness: The Hidden Role of Chance in Life and in the Markets.* The "blindspot" metaphor of these titles may come from the experience of driving a car. In ophthalmology the Greek word *scotoma* is used, as it is also in the study of cognition: see Bernard Lonergan, *Insight: A Study of Human Understanding* (New York: Philosophical Library / Longmans, 1958), 191.

54   Benjamin Nugent, "The Adulterous Sins of Our Father Figures," *The New York Times,* April 27, 2013.

55   John Henry Newman, *Arians of the Fourth Century* (London and New York: Longmans, Green, 3rd edition, 1871), 23.

56   Ibid., 33.

57   I am indebted for several of these quotations to a presentation on the thought of John Henry Newman given by Michael Paul Gallagher, SJ, at Georgetown University, September 24, 2010.

58   Richard Wagner, *Opera and Drama* (University of Nebraska Press, 1995), 209. Also quoted by Daniel Barenboim, "Wagner and the Jews," *The New York Review of Books,* June 20, 2013.

59   See John Cassidy, "He Foresaw the End of an Era," *The New York Review of Books* October 23, 2008.

60   Amos Tversky and Daniel Kahneman, "Judgment Under Uncertainty: Heuristics and Biases," *Science* 185:4157, 1974.

61   Most recently in Kahneman's *Thinking Fast and Slow* (NY: Farrar, Straus and Giroux, 2011).

62   Erica Goode, "On Profit, Loss and the Mysteries of the Mind," *The New York Times* November 5, 2002.

63   Goode, Ibid.

64   Freeman Dyson, "How to Dispel Your Illusions," *The New York Review of Books* December 22, 2011.

65   Ferdinand Mount, "When Our World Turned Upside Down," review of Christian Caryl, *Strange Rebels: 1979 and the Birth of the 21st Century, The New York Review of Books,* June 20, 2013.

66   Jonathan F. S. Post, ed., *The Selected Letters of Anthony Hecht* (Baltimore: Johns Hopkins University Press, 2012), 250. Also quoted by Edward Mendelsohn, "Seeing Is Not Believing," review of Hecht's *Selected Poems* and *Selected Letters, The New York Review of Books* June 20, 2013.

67   Kevin Roberts of Saatchi & Saatchi, on the PBS show "The Persuaders," *Frontline,* 2004.

68   Emily Eakin, "Penetrating the Mind by Metaphor," *The New York Times* February 23, 2002.

69   Charles Duhigg, "How Companies Learn Your Secrets," *The New York Times* February 16, 2012.

70   Robert Penn Warren, *All The King's Men*. (New York: Houghton Mifflin Harcourt, 2006), 106.

71   Ronan Farrow on MSNBC's "The Cycle," October 29, 2013.

72   Commentator on MSNBC July 26, 2013.

73   Mark Danner, "The Politics of Fear," *The New York Review of Books* November 22, 2012.

74   New York: Hyperion, 2009.

75   New York: Hyperion, 2007.

76   Mark Danner, op. cit.

77   Garry Wills, "American Adam," *The New York Review of Books,* March 6, 1997.

78   "Age-old": for historical perspective, see David Hackett Fischer, *Albion's Seed* (New York: Oxford University Press, 1989).

79   Drew Westen, "What Happened to Obama's Passion?" *The New York Times Magazine* August 6, 2011.

80   Yes, President Obama cites tales of people who have been treated unfairly or who have triumphed over adversity, but to my ear these have the feel of "proof-text" exemplifications of a policy abstractly conceived.

81   Editor's note: Then-presidential candidate Michele Bachmann in a January 2011 speech.

82   William P. Sampson, SJ, *The Earliest Church* (forthcoming from New Academia, Spring 2016), chapter 11.

83   Gene Weingarten, "God, That's Funny," *The Washington Post,* April 4, 1999.

84   Anthony Trollope, *Linda Tressel* (New York: Oxford University Press).

85   New York: Samuel French.

86   Henry St. John, Viscount Bolingbroke, "Authority in Matters of Religion," *The Works of Lord Bolingbroke* (London: A.M. Kelley, 1967), Vol. III, 406.

87   The sentence is unexceptionable if "within" is meant as "embodied in," "inseparable from." But if so, the preposition is having to do some heavy lifting.

88   My translation.

89   In the King James Version, "Thou art the man," whence the title of this book. [Editor's note: "Thou Art the Man" was his original title for this book, but he discarded it in favor of the current one.]

90   The Pharisees have had a bad press, and the bad image we have of them makes it hard to put ourselves in the place of Jesus' original audience. Hearing the parable we tend to identify with the tax collector, and

imaginatively distance ourselves from the Pharisee, since we know how the story ends, with the tax collector "justified." My friend the Jesuit New Testament scholar John R. Donahue has pointed out that by so distancing ourselves from the Pharisee we are being "pharisaic."

91   Charles Dickens, *Hard Times*, chapter 2.

92   John R. Donahue, SJ, *America*, July 1-8, 2002.

93   *The Habit of Being, Letters of Flannery O'Connor*, Sally Fitzgerald ed. (New York: Farrar Straus & Giroux, 1979), Letter to Ben Griffith, May 4, 1955; 79. She also wrote "To the hard of hearing you shout, and for the almost blind you draw large and startling figures." Brainard Cheney, "Flannery O'Connor's Campaign for Her Country," Sewanee Review, 72 (Autumn, 1964), 555-58. In C. Ralph Stephens, ed. *Correspondence of Flannery O'Connor and the Brainard Cheneys*, Appendix E, 213.

94   Walker Percy, "Notes for a Novel about the End of the World" in *The Message in the Bottle: How Queer Man Is, How Queer Language Is, and What One Has to Do with the Other* (New York: Farrar, Straus & Giroux, 1975), 118.

95   William Barrett in *The Atlantic*, July 1965. http://www.theatlantic.com/magazine/archive/1965/07/flannery-oconnor-review/309545/

96   "Jesus sees life through the eyes of the *"anawim*, the poor and humble of the land." John R. Donahue, op. cit. Nowadays, one speaks of "the preferential option for the poor."

97   Flannery O'Connor, *Wise Blood* (New York: New American Library, 1983), 10.

98   Concluding an early-May meeting of the faculty, the president of the faculty senate thanked all for their attendance and participation in the meeting at a very crowded time of the academic year, despite the inconvenience: "You have the satisfaction of knowing you were there on Saint Crispin's Day." Puzzled faculty reactions included "Is today St. Crispin's Day!" and "Who is St. Crispin?" I guess they had never read or seen *Henry V*.

99   Its web site tells us that IARPA "invests in high-risk, high-payoff research programs that have the potential to provide the United States with an overwhelming intelligence advantage over future adversaries."

100   IARPA, "Cultural Insights From the Use of Metaphors Program," Request for Information, closed September 9, 2009.

101   *Dives* is the Latin for "rich" and over the centuries the adjective has been made the proper name of the rich man; the other character in the parable does have a name, Lazarus.

102   Clarity and precision are to be esteemed, of course, hard-won values that they are, but they are far from being the whole story.

103   It also lends itself to the supposed disjunction between, and separability of, substance and style. For a lucid and compelling treatment

of this question see John W. O'Malley, S.J., *What Happened at Vatican II?* (Cambridge, Mass.: Harvard University Press, 2008), 305-313.

104 Billy Collins, "Introduction to Poetry," from *The Apple that Astonished Paris.* (University of Arkansas Press, 1988).

105 Adam Kirsch, "Extracting the Woodchuck," *Harvard Magazine* January-February 2014.

106 *Souls of Black Folk* (Henry Louis Gates, Jr., ed.; New York: Oxford University Press, 2007), 3. See also Alford A. Young, Jr., "The Soul of *The Philadelphia Negro* and *The Souls of Black Folk,* in Alford A. Young, Jr., ed., *The Souls of W.E.B. DuBois* (Boulder, Colorado: Paradigm, 2006), 63-66.

107 *The New York Times Magazine* April 13, 2008.

108 I disagree with former Senator Rick Santorum on pretty much every topic, political and religious, but he has been the victim of the kind of confusions I have been treating here, salted with mean-spiritedness. The Supreme Court in *Lawrence v. Texas* extended the right to privacy to consensual sexual activity. Santorum said the decision was so broadly drawn that no form of sexual activity could be proscribed or regulated by law. He gave some examples, including bestiality, of sexual acts that the decision would leave inviolate. Critics ignored the "proportions" of the comment and descended to the particulars. Santorum never compared homosexual acts to acts of bestiality. He has been traduced by this vicious misconstrual of his words.

109 See George Santayana's description of "love" quoted in chapter 6 above.

110 It was part of Disability Awareness Week in early April 1990, organized by a student group, led by a senior Nursing student, Dina Anfuso, called Challenge Georgetown.

111 One student put it well: "There's no way to tell what a disability is like." Emphasis on "tell."

112 At Georgetown University, "Wounded Warriors" returning from service in Iraq and Afghanistan are given the opportunity to use their skills and learn new ones in an academic credit-earning program run by the School of Continuing Education. An important part of the experience is a course offering, taught by Father Richard Curry, SJ, that focuses on dramatic monologue. Each veteran is taught to re-create his or her deployment experience by writing and delivering their story. Writing and re-writing and then oral presentation before the class serves many purposes in the life of the returning service member. "Story" and story-telling are heart of the program. It is therapeutic for the veterans, and opens the imaginations of the undergraduates in the course to a world of experience—pain, hope against hope, courage, redemption—they could never imagine on their own.

Besides the in-class experience, there is a practical, entrepreneurial component, centered in the Dogtag Bakery: to quote from the Web site, "Veterans will operate the bakery: learning skills from baking to sales to business management. At the same time, they will pursue a course of study focusing on small business administration and entrepreneurship, providing each student with the skills needed for the successful pursuit of a job or a foundation to create a small business venture of their own." (www.dogtagbakery.org)

113 Flannery O'Connnor's character Hazel Motes again: he wanted the security of his hometown, "with his two eyes open, and his hands always handling the familiar thing, his feet on the known track." op. cit.

114 *The Mighty From Their Thrones: Power in the Biblical Tradition* (Philadelphia: Fortress, 1987), 9.

115 Fintan O'Toole, "Guns in the Family," Review of Joseph O'Neill, *Blood-Dark Track: A Family History*, *The New York Review of Books* April 11, 2002. I think of images from Little Rock and Birmingham. After the September 1963 church bombing that killed four little girls, a preacher, the Reverend Connie Lynch, founder of the National States Rights Party, preached the word that "the four young girls had been 'old enough to have venereal diseases' and were no more human or innocent than rattlesnakes. 'So I kill 'em all,' he shouted, 'and if it's four less niggers tonight, then good for whoever planted the bomb. We're all better off.'" Russell Baker, review of Taylor Branch, *Pillar of Fire*, *The New York Review of Books* April 9, 1998. (Maybe I should have included the Reverend Connie Lynch in chapter 5, "Imagining Others.")

116 O'Toole, "Guns." op. cit.

117 Vincent Crapanzano, "A Reporter at Large: Waiting," *The New Yorker*, March 18, 1985.

118 Harvey Cox, in *Harvard Divinity Bulletin*, reprinted in Gary MacEoin, ed. *The Papacy and the People of God* (Orbis Books, 1998), 154.

119 *Spiritual Exercises* §22. ". . . se ha de presuponer que todo buen cristiano ha de ser más prompto a salvar la proposición del prójimo que a condenarla; y si no puede salvar, inquira cómo la entiende, . . .

120 See Irénée Hausherr, *Penthos: The Doctrine of Compunction in the Christian East* (Kalamazoo, Michigan: Cistercian Publications, 1982).

121 *Spiritual Exercises* §60.

122 Ibid. §104: haciéndome yo un pobrecito y esclavito indigno.

123 As suggested earlier, some prefer to speak of the "guide" rather than the "director" of a retreat. "Directed retreat" or "guided retreat" are terms that distinguish it from a "preached retreat," where the dynamic—a series of allocutions and sermons imparted to a congregation—is very different from what I am describing here.

124 William P. Sampson, SJ, "Contemplating a Mystery," notes for retreatants. The term "mystery" here and in the text comes from Ignatius in the book of the *Spiritual Exercises*. It refers to what Jesus does and says in the Gospel narratives.

125 Both expressions are euphemisms for the real, the proper and precise (and biblical), term, "enemy." Most retreatants would be shocked to be told they have an enemy, but "charity problem" makes the medicine go down easy.

126 Matthew 11:12.

127 I find it amusing if not instructive to change channels from MS-NBC to EWTN (the "Catholic" television network) and hear the same tone of voice on each. The one speaks of women's reproductive rights in a serenely apodictic tone used when speaking of an issue long settled; the other speaks the same way, but to opposite effect. Each is professing its faith.

128 Macaulay, "History," from *The Miscellaneous Works of Lord Macaulay* (New York: Harper, 1880), 193.

129 Rowan Williams, Archbishop of Canterbury, at a "Building Bridges" conference held at Georgetown University, said that deepening understanding "is not about finding a common core at all. It is about finding the appropriate language in which differences can be talked about rather than used as an excuse for violent separation." March 29, 2004. Full text available at his website, http://rowanwilliams.archbishopofcanterbury.org/articles.php/1211/analysing-atheism-unbelief-and-the-world-of-faiths.

130 Jasper Griffin, "The Myth of Myths," *The New York Review of Books* November 4, 1999; and exchanges with correspondents in subsequent issues, January 20, 2000, and June 15, 2000.

131 Matthew 5:44-48, my translation.

132 James 1:23-24.

CPSIA information can be obtained
at www.ICGtesting.com
Printed in the USA
FFOW05n2120031215